I AM NOT A MISTAKE, I AM MEANT TO BE

Healing to Cleanse the Residue of Sexual Abuse

Garlena L. Hines

Author's Note:

*T*hroughout this book you will notice that the name of our soul's enemy appears in lowercase. I have decided to refuse to give him any credit to the extent that I am willing to violate grammatical rules.

To contact Evangelist Hines for speaking engagements, click on *www.glhinesministries.com*.

"This powerful book sheds the light of God's truth in every dark place, where satan lurks in the lives of those who have faced sexual abuse. It ministers the redemptive power of Jesus Christ to those longing to walk in wholeness, victory, and new life. Readers will be changed forever by the words and testimony of Evangelist Hines. Read this book and allow her to usher you into the healing, deliverance, and transforming power of Jesus Christ. These God-inspired words will free you from hurt, guilt, shame, and fear such that you, too, will discover that *"You are not a mistake, you are meant to be."*

Hope D. Blackwell
Author and Teacher

"There are untold numbers of people whose lives are defined by dysfunctional behaviors, which stem from the emotional upheaval of their lives' situations. It is not by accident that God has positioned Evangelist Hines to tell her story for such a time as this. The enemy has deceived many into living out false beliefs about themselves, as a result of lies spoken into them by ill-meaning individuals and through situations designed to wound and cripple their spirits.

Garlena Hines has been given a message of deliverance to set the captives free! She is an anointed woman of God, inspired by the Holy Spirit to expose the enemy's strategy to trap people in a lifecycle of pain and dysfunction. Filled with hope and restored by the truth of God's Word, you can find wholeness and peace as you embrace this powerful message.

Dr. Neal R. Siler, Ph.D.
Pastor and Teacher

> *"He sent His word, and healed them, and delivered them from their destructions."*
> **Psalms 107:20 (KJV)**

"I am both very honored and humbled to have the privilege to offer a few words regarding this wonderful publication! Time has proven over and over again that the art of writing outlives all other arts and technologies. Long playing records and recorded tapes have been replaced by new technologies that will themselves be replaced. Yet the works of Shakespeare and the masters are still ever-fresh. We will forever treasure the writings of a man who led his people out of centuries of bondage, an apostle who wrote letters from prison, and an old man banished to an island, writing to seven churches.

"This book will have a long life also. Evangelist Hines has been open and transparent enough to cause all who will read this book to see the One in her—the One who has walked her through every step of her life. The words that she has written were given to her by God. They really are His. He has sent them through this book to heal those who are in need of healing and wholeness after the storms of their lives. God's words in this book will also deliver those who feel that they only face destruction because of the pain they have endured. Power is born of pain, and ministry is born of misery. As happy as I am about my covenant sister's first book, I am so much happier for the multiplied multitudes that will be blessed by owning and reading it!"

Dr. A. Ray Rouson, Sr.
Pastor Emeritus, First Pentecostal United Holy Church, Norfolk, Virginia, 2nd Vice President, Virginia District Convocation, United Holy Church of America, Inc.

DEDICATION

This book is dedicated to the many women who have been victims of sexual abuse. For the woman who is still haunted by the memories of the abuse and who finds herself unable to move on, I pray that she finds endurance. For the rape victim who's been traumatized, I pray she finds peace. For the woman who is still trapped in yesterday, because someone she trusted violated her as a child, I pray that she finds the strength to move forward. I pray that through these writings and the sharing of my own struggles with sexual abuse, you will all find the healing you need and so that the yokes of bondage can be broken from your minds, enabling you to walk in your divine destinies. Be whole and free, knowing that you are not a mistake, you are meant to be.

I especially dedicate this book to the memory of my late pastor, Bishop Thomas E. Talley. I'm grateful for the teachings and love provided to me under your leadership.

ACKNOWLEDGEMENTS

First and foremost, I acknowledge and thank God who rests, rules, and consumes my life. I feel so blessed that God has released me to share my testimony through this book. I write in loving memory of my parents, Garland Bruce and Mary Louise Hines, my God-mother, Mrs Carlene Myrick and my twins, Angelica Nicole and James Adrian: I wish you all could have lived to witness this great moment in my life.

To my siblings, Jeanette, David, Linda, Cheryle, Aaron and June, thank you for believing in me and for encouraging me to write this book. To the staff of G. L. Hines Ministries, Von Art Productions, Click-It-Twice LLC, and Eyes of Elegance Photography, I praise God for your being a part of the awesome assignment God has given me to spread the gospel of Jesus Christ. To the "Holy Ghost Posse," we have prayed, cried, and labored together through some serious warfare, and I thank you for being there for me. To the Grove Baptist Church family and the Keepers of the Flame ministerial staff, thank you for continuing to support my ministry with your love, support, and prayers. To my spiritual father and Pastor, Dr. Melvin O. Marriner, you are the best pastor this side of heaven. Thanks for preaching the Word that caused me to move from "Vision to Destiny." To all of my co-laborers in the gospel, pastors, friends, mentors, family, and my dearest cousin and "best friend" MSgt (Ret) Michael Potts, I could not have done this without your help.

To my beautiful daughter—God's vessel of honor—Ms. Loneka, I am so proud of you, and I thank God that you are becoming the young lady He's ordained you to be. Thank you for helping me cross this milestone and for being supportive through the writing of this book.

Lastly, to my enemies, thank you for giving me a reason to grow stronger. To the haters, thank you for giving me a reason to become more determined. To those who abused me, thank you for giving me something over which I could gain victory.

I praise God for all of you!

FOREWORD

The groundbreaking message of truth, hope, and wholeness through pain and suffering will undoubtedly shatter the bonds of depression, shame, and guilt. Evangelist Garlena Hines passionately reveals a heart-wrenching journey through self-destruction propelled by physical violation, emotional manipulation, and demonic deception. Her constant quest for deliverance and forgiveness through the emancipated "Word of God" has now become an example of restoration and fulfillment.

Mark Twain wrote, "Plan for the future because that's where you are going to spend the rest of your life." Evangelist Hines leads us to embrace purpose while being liberated from past curses and false perceptions. Reading this book will seem as though someone has thrown you a lifeline while you were drowning in the Atlantic Ocean. Her honest and open transparency through a turbulent process will offer you hope and a desire to reach for your God-given destiny.

The spiritual and practical testimony is absolutely fascinating! Her life's experience will indeed bless the Kingdom and you. Read it and celebrate.

Melvin O. Marriner, M. Div., D. Min.
Senior Pastor
Grove Baptist Church

CONTENTS

CHAPTER ONE

How It All Began...

MY "BOOGIE MAN"

Growing up in the seventies, my friends and I were always afraid of the so-called "boogie man." For many of us, the boogie man was a stranger who hid in the closet or behind a tree. The overall fear was that the boogie man was someone who would hurt us. If we saw an unfamiliar man walking in the neighborhood, all of the kids would run and yell, "The boogie man is coming!" If we saw the neighborhood drunk staggering toward us, we would run home screaming, "The boogie man is coming!" Well, my boogie man was our sixteen-year-old neighbor, Gary. He was different from the other boys, who seemed to be afraid of their parents—they at least showed respect. Gary, however, seemed to have his own rules when it came to respecting others. I can't remember a time when he actually attended school, and if my memory serves me correctly, he was a high-school dropout.

Gary was very aggressive and was involved in many altercations with the neighborhood kids and with his own siblings, as well. He was very direct, and if he felt like saying something, he did. Now, this might cause one to think that Gary was from an unruly family—one that did not teach proper morals and values. In fact, just the opposite was true. His mother was a Godly woman, who loved the Lord and His Word. She taught her children about God, and love was in the air of their home. His mother and mine were best friends; we all attended the same church and worked in ministry together. My sister and I played with his sisters, and he would often spend time with my brother. Despite his problems and bad behavior, our families got along great.

During this era (the 70s), everyone in the community partici-pated in raising the neighborhood's children. If you were misbe-having and a neighbor who knew the values of your family saw you, they would chastise you and send you home for more discipline. As friends, we slept at each others' homes quite often, and because many of us were not fortunate enough to live in big homes, we often all slept together in the same bed, on the living room floor, or wher-ever we felt comfortable. It was also pretty common for the mother of the house to throw us all in the bathtub together, and we all took turns sitting at the stove to get our hair hot-combed.

These were good times for most, but for me it was a time filled with fear of the boogie man. Because we kids were allowed to go in and out of each others' homes, there were times when things would happen that the parents would be unaware of. We all thought that we could and should trust our families, friends, and neighbors, as during that time, reports of child molestation, murders, black-on-black crime, and even school suspensions were rare.

I was the tender age of five when I first encountered my boogie man. Saturday mornings, I loved to wake up early and watch "Road Runner" cartoons. I always had faith that the coyote would actu-ally catch the Road Runner, but of course, that never happened. My mother and siblings would still be asleep when the show aired, but I was old enough to go downstairs, turn on the TV, and watch quietly so as not to wake anyone. One Saturday morning, Gary came over looking for my brother. Now, for some reason, Gary would sleep all day during the week, but he could manage to get up early on Saturday morning to pay our family a visit.

This particular morning, he came over and watched "Road Runner" with me, which I didn't think was strange at all. As we watched, Gary began to tickle me, telling me to keep quiet so no one would hear. He asked for some water, and when I proceeded toward the kitchen, he walked behind me and began to fondle me. He tried to make me believe it was just a joke, but even in my child's mind, I knew something was not right. I cannot begin to tell you the fear I felt. We sat back down in front of the TV and he put his hand up my pajama top. I was terrified of the way he touched me. I was a chunky, five-year-old little girl who had not developed anything that should have aroused anyone, but Gary was determined. He demanded that I be quiet, and told me that if I wasn't, he would kill everyone in the house.

Was it possible that he could do that? I didn't know, but I wasn't willing to take the risk of finding out. I didn't want to be the cause of another death in my family. After all, I had been told that I was the cause of my father's death, and I just couldn't take the risk. My father had died when my mother was six months pregnant with me. I'd never heard her discuss his death, so from time to time, I would ask my siblings about what seemed to be a mystery death. My brother—being mean as brothers can be—told me that my father had killed himself because he knew I was coming and he didn't want me. Thus, in my five-year-old mind, I had to save my mother from dying if my father had indeed killed himself. (I was later to learn that my father had passed due to a massive heart attack.) Nevertheless, I did what Gary told me to do—I kept quiet, sat there, and let him fondle me.

As a five-year-old, I didn't know what sexual feelings were. I didn't know how to respond or how to feel. I do remember being kissed and slobbered upon that Saturday morning. It was very uncomfortable and it felt nasty. I sat there wishing that my brother would come down and catch him, but that never happened. My boogie man had found me, and I was now his victim.

The abuse continued quietly. Gary had discovered that he had free reign over me, and he would often ask me if I knew when my mother would be away or when she would be at church. I always thought that was strange, especially since our mothers belonged to the same church. Most times, I'd answer, "I don't know," but that never kept him away. Eventually, I became so fearful that I would follow my brother around just to protect myself from Gary. This began the development of my "internal defense mechanism," with which I still struggle today. If I feel that someone may hurt me, I find a way to protect myself. I didn't have this mechanism perfected back in the early seventies, however. I only had fear. I began wetting the bed, which today is one of the signs indicating that a child might be experiencing stress. However, during the seventies, it was a sign of laziness, so I was reprimanded.

So here I was—a five-year-old bed-wetter, who no one knew was being molested. I thought, *God when will this stop?* Some child molesters are gentle and will try to make the child feel comfortable, but Gary was always rough with me. There were times when he penetrated my vaginal areas with as many fingers as he could. Can you imagine that happening to a five-year-old? Afterward, I often experienced vaginal soreness and severe pain while urinating, but who could I tell? I thought, *Maybe Gary will understand that he's hurting me and stop.*

By the time I was six, I was being molested at least twice a week. It had become such a routine that whenever he came over, I no longer fought him and I no longer looked for refuge. No one could see the anxiety that overcame me when he was around or see the drastic change in my behavior. I remember one night, as I was battling a bad cold, I heard an advertisement for a new movie called *Mark of the Devil.* I was terrified of that commercial because it was so morbid. I lie in bed crying out of fear, and instead of my brother coming to check on me, he sent Gary. That was the most horrifying night ever. I was bedridden with a fever, running nose, and chills, and still this young man came in trying to fondle and penetrate me. I tried to resist, but I was so full of fear that I couldn't even scream. He tried to make me touch him, and when I refused he became very angry. *Would he move from molestation to rape?* I thought it was possible. When I finally managed to get a scream out, my brother ran into the room and asked, "What are you doing to my sister?" Gary made up a story, telling my brother that the radio had been left on. He told him that I'd screamed because of the commercial. Then he proceeded to pull the covers over me and kiss me goodnight. *Had I missed something? Isn't this the same boy who had just tried to rape me? How can he now tuck me in and kiss me goodnight?*

THE BOOGIE MAN IS GONE

For two years I endured Gary's abuse. It had become a part of my life and had caused me to begin acting out in unusual ways. When my cousins came over, I no longer wanted to play hopscotch, 1-2-3 red light, or hide and seek. I wanted to play "doctor and nurse" or "husband and wife." I had begun acting out what I had been introduced to and was now trying to expose others to it. I wanted to be the doctor who had to "examine" private body parts, because I had been exposed to perversion. I wanted to be the wife and show my cousins what Gary had taught me by molesting me. I had been introduced to feelings that I was too young to understand, and now I was behaving in an unnatural way. *Was this how my life would be? Had the boogie man perverted me for good?*

By the time I reached seven years old, however, my boogie man was gone. I'm not sure what happened to him; I just know that I didn't see him anymore, and I felt free from the torture of those two years. I enjoyed the remainder of my second-grade school year in peace. No one bothered me; no one was pulling on my "imaginary breasts," fondling me, or kissing on me, trying to fulfill some perverted desire. I was finally free—well, temporarily.

THE BOOGIE MAN BECOMES THE "BOOGIE WOMAN"

I felt like I could finally live life as a normal seven-year-old with Gary gone. Things were returning to normal, and I thought that if I tried real hard, I could forget what he'd done to me. I decided to become more involved in my church's activities. Since my mother was so active in the church, we kids were not allowed to simply attend; we also had to participate. I didn't like the idea of being an usher and passing out fans, so I decided to sing in the choir. After all, my mother had a family singing group that often sung on Sunday afternoons at different churches. So I figured that being in the choir would continue to develop my vocal gifts and talents.

My mother loved people, and the kids at church loved to come over to our house after morning worship. At the church we attended, we were sure to have an afternoon service, and since we lived a block from the church, it was pretty common for kids to come over until the afternoon service began. One particular young lady who loved to come over was Regina. She was being raised by her father and didn't have much contact with her other siblings. I think it had become overwhelming for this man to raise his daughter; young girls can sometimes be difficult to understand, and it must have been a challenge to explain and witness all the changes his daughter would undergo as she matured. So, Regina spent a lot of time with my family. Very soon after starting to hang out with her, I discovered that Regina also loved playing "husband and wife." She didn't like playing with my male cousins, but she loved playing this game with me. I couldn't understand why she preferred me, but despite my hesitation, we played anyway.

At first, we just pretended that we were husband and wife with children. I had lots of dolls, so we used them as our kids. However, this wasn't enough for Regina. She wanted us to really pretend we were married. Because Regina was a little older than me, my mother would allow her to babysit me if I was allowed to miss an afternoon church service. Initially, this was fun, because we would eat junk food and watch TV. But very soon, being around Regina became stressful. Because she was older, she was more developed. She would have conversations with me about her body that I knew were inappropriate, and when I refused to partake in them or listen, I would be physically abused. *Here we go again*, I thought. I'd figured that when Gary disappeared, the abuse had ended for good. I was wrong. When Regina didn't get her way with me, she would become violent and aggressive. She would twist my arm and throw me under the kitchen table if I refused to touch her. After a while, I knew she would beat me up, so I thought it best to just give in.

Regretting it the entire time—hoping someone would catch her—I felt like I was being tormented. I thought that if someone would see her hitting me, I could at least make an escape. But that never happened. Eventually, I began to hate the suggestion seeing Regina; however, I could offer no reason to my mother that I thought she would believe as to why I didn't want to be around Regina. In one of her rages against me, Regina kneed me in my groin area and it caused me a lot of pain and left a bruise. Finally, I had a reason to tell my mother—I had proof! The next Sunday came, and when it was time for me to go over Regina's house, I showed my mother the bruise and told her that Regina had beaten me up. I was rescued from further beatings, but had I spoken up too late? After all, she'd been abusing me for at least a year; I had been officially introduced to lesbianism. *Will I grow up to desire women? Will I live a normal life? What else could possibly happen to me?* I didn't have the answers to those questions, but I knew one thing at that point: I was free from my abusers—*or was I?*

CHAPTER TWO

I Was His Tamar

*"But as she was feeding him, he grabbed her and demanded,
'Come to bed with me, my darling sister.' ... But Amnon wouldn't
listen to her, and since he was stronger than she was, he raped
her."*
II Samuel 13: 11, 14 (NLT)

While the story of Amnon raping his half sister Tamar is not the only controversial story in the Bible, it is one of the most familiar accounts of incest. Amnon was vexed, or filled, with lust for Tamar and desired her in a way that was unnatural. His quest to conquer her grew intense, and he was encouraged by his friend Jonadab to pretend that he was ill. Upon receiving this bad advice, Amnon put this deceptive plan into action. He sent for his sister Tamar, who became concerned about his health, and asked her to cook for him. Fulfilling her brother's request, she cooked his meal. While she did so, he made an advance at her, and then raped her. What had been in Amnon that caused him to do this to his sister? Had he been molested, or was this a generational curse of lust descending from his father's desire for women? What was it about Tamar that made him desire her so strongly? I have often asked similar questions upon hearing about other rape cases—but who really can understand the mind of an attacker?

As I entered my pre-teenage years, I no longer had to worry about Gary or Regina. They had become distant memories to me, and after being free from abuse for about three years, I had gotten to the age where my mother would soon be having that "little talk" with me—preparing me to deal with the opposite sex and other important issues of life. While going through this particular stage, I discovered that I had some serious issues that no one seemed to be able to explain. I had previously been a happy-go-lucky little girl, but somehow I'd developed an attitude filled with so much rage and anger that I often engaged in physical violence against others. Regardless of the person or the incident, I often found reasons to fight with other children. Many times, the kids in my neighborhood and church refused to have anything to do with me because of these rageful outbursts. No one could explain the reason, but my mother made sure that I was at the altar so that I could have the "evil cast out of me" during prayer services. No one thought that maybe I needed a male presence in my life, since my father was dead and my brother was off doing his own thing, or that I'd been through some traumatic experiences.

The year was 1977, and many of the teens at church were becoming friends, hanging out with each other, and having fun. But because of my bad behavior, many of them had no desire to befriend me. They had sleepovers and parties to which I was not invited because of my behavior. I remember wishing, *If only someone would understand my pain, maybe I could be a better person.*

Sunday, July 3, 1977 was the luckiest day of my life—or so I thought. Out of all the women in the church, someone had chosen me. Had I finally found a boyfriend my age from church or school? No, I was being set up again for another round of sexual abuse. This time, it involved my cousin James—a handsome young man with a beautiful wife and two children. His first daughter had been adopted, and after years of trying, his second child had been born in February of 1977. Most people thought he had it all. He had completed twenty years in the military, an ordained deacon and was employed with a naval facility; life seemed to be going pretty well for him. But something was missing in his life. What that something was, I don't

26

know, but for some reason he wanted to be with me. *Was this really a desire or was it a perversion that was suddenly stirring?*

For months he would compliment me, tickle me, and kiss me on the cheek. Some of these kisses even found their way to my lips. I felt so special. After all, I was not liked very much at school, at church, in my neighborhood, or in my family, so this was just the attention I thought I needed. I was going through puberty and trying to understand who I was—but I was still sucking my thumb and wetting the bed. Many of my peers knew that I was a bed-wetter, and thus I was often the butt of many jokes. But when James began paying special attention to me, it changed everything. I would often dream of us getting married and moving away from everyone. I even went so far as reading a book entitled *Kissing Cousins.* Somehow that book had turned up in our staunch Pentecostal house, and I'd gotten my hands on it. After reading it, I concluded that since James had kissed me like the man had kissed his cousin in the book, he must love me.

I was no longer irritated by attending so many church services, because I knew James would be there. I remember seeking just the right seat in church so that I would be able see him, and often he would wink at me, showing me special attention. I would melt in my seat, thinking, *This handsome man really loves me.* Now, although we were in a Pentecostal church, not all of the women were "saved." Many of them also developed crushes—inappropriate affection and feelings toward him. You see, he was a quiet man, but when he entered a room, he attracted everyone's attention—including mine. I remember feeling like Cinderella when she won the heart of the prince over her step-sisters. I would often daydream while sitting in church, and although I knew the thoughts were not Godly, I didn't know enough to understand that thoughts of lust had begun entering my mind. My thoughts were limited to hugging, patting, and kissing, but they were just enough to open the door for the enemy. It never crossed my mind that being in a relationship with James would be incestuous or wrong at all. I simply felt that we were two cousins who loved each other in a different way. Truthfully, I didn't know what love was; I didn't understand sexual feelings, and I really didn't know what I was getting into. All I knew was that he'd chosen me.

HE MADE HIS MOVE

"So Amnon lay down and pretended to be sick. And when the king came to see him, Amnon asked him, 'Please let my sister Tamar come and cook my favorite dish as I watch. Then I can eat it from her own hands.'"
II Samuel 13:6 (NLT)

The Bible states that Amnon had a very crafty friend who advised him to pretend he was sick and to then summon Tamar. Out of her love and respect for Amnon, Tamar fulfilled his request, and even today, many attackers act in the same manner. They win the trust of their victims before committing the crime. They often talk with their victims, trying to make them feel comfortable by sharing personal information. This helps them to gain the confidence of their intended victim, so that when the victim least expects, the predator can make his move.

Every second Sunday, we would have a youth program at church. I guess this was the time for all of us to show how talented we were. It was fun, and it kept us off the streets. Normally after these services, James would volunteer to take me home, even though I only lived a couple of blocks away. Because it was normally dark by the time service was over, my mother would consent; she figured I'd be traveling home safely. One particular Sunday night, as James was taking me home, we realized that no one was in the house. I did not have a key, so I had to wait until someone returned. Usually, during times like this, I would go to 7-Eleven and get a Slurpee. Summer days and nights were hot and humid, so we kept cool anyway we could.

Well, James didn't feel that it was right to make me wait for my mother alone, so we headed toward 7-Eleven together. As we traveled, I noticed something—he was holding my hand and rubbing it until I began to feel a sensation that I'd never felt before. I didn't know what was going on, but I knew it felt good. When we returned to my home, we discovered that still no one had returned. So we drove around and ended up at a local place where we could walk on the pier and talk of taking a cruise somewhere. As we walked, I noticed that James was limping. He said he needed to lean on me because his leg was bothering him. We hugged, as all of the couples were doing, as we walked the boardwalk. *Could this be the "Amnon syndrome?" —with him pretending to be ill so that I could be at his side?*

We walked for a while and then returned to the car, because he claimed that his leg was in great pain. As we sat in the car talking, I began to ask questions: "Do you think I'm cute?" "Do you think I'm fat?" "Do you like other women in the church, or do you like me?" As I asked these childish questions, he responded with every answer I wanted to hear—he was winning me over. *Wow, could it be true that he's really choosing me?* The conversation continued and he kissed me on the left cheek, then the right, then on my chin, my forehead, and finally on my lips.

I felt like I'd won a million dollars. I fell back in the seat and said, "I can't believe you did that!" He asked, "Do you want me to do it again?" I told him I did, and this time when he kissed me, it was not a peck on the lips; it was a long, intimate kiss. Those feelings I'd felt when he rubbed my hand became even more intense. Later, while he was driving me home, I sat on the passenger side of that Buick Regal thinking I was the luckiest girl in the world, but as he drove me home he said, "You can't tell anybody what's happened; this is our secret." At once, my smile turned into a frown, because I wanted everyone to know that I had found my "true love." I didn't like what he'd said, but I agreed to it. I felt that since he was older, he probably knew what was best. That night I slept like a baby, holding my pillow and feeling like I had been crowned Miss America and that there was nothing I could not conquer. Needless to say, that kiss marked the beginning of years of confusion, perversion, and pain in my life.

THE SEEDS WERE PLANTED

While many of the girls at school talked about their boyfriends, I sat quietly, thinking about my secret relationship with an older man who had his own car, money, and home—a man who could take care of me. Despite being desired by the other women in the church, he'd chosen to be with me. What I didn't realize was that my cousin had planted a seed of perversion and confusion in my life. He had also introduced me to the spirit of "being the concubine" or "being the other woman." Regardless of our kinship, he was married and spending inappropriate time with a female other than his wife.

Because I couldn't tell anyone about this relationship, I had to lie to my mother, my siblings, and my friends to see James. Most times we would plan to meet each other after Bible studies, after Sunday night services, or following any other special service at our church. Since I was not giving my mother any serious problems and was always attending church, she trusted me. I lied depending on what James wanted to do or where he wanted to take me. I told my mother many times that I was visiting friends that didn't exist, and I also learned to lie about attending church services that I never attended or that never existed. My only desire was to find a way to meet James after church. It didn't matter if he drove me from church to our favorite spot or if I had to meet him somewhere; I just wanted to be with him. I had become an expert in lying and walking in deception. The seed had been planted. *"For he that soweth to his flesh shall of the flesh reap corruption; but he that soweth to the Spirit shall of the Spirit reap life everlasting,"* (Galatians 6:8 [KJV]).

I was learning early to sow to my flesh, and my flesh was being corrupted daily. I no longer desired to attend church to hear the Word or to fellowship with others. Instead, I desired to go to church so that I could see my lover and fellowship with him. I was getting more deeply involved, and my flesh was being pleased. I was young and inexperienced, and I wanted to show James that I could be a woman. How could I do this when I was only twelve? These were the most impressionable years of my life, the years where I would make the decision to be a leader or a follower. I should have been growing into my own identity, learning about myself, choosing my friends, and spending time with my family. Instead, I was trying to learn ways to please a forty-two-year-old man. I missed out much of my childhood, because my focus was on pleasing James: from the way I twisted my ponytails to the dresses I chose to wear each Sunday. After all, I didn't want him to lose interest in me and find someone else. I became obsessed with looking good and making sure he complimented me when he saw me. Since I couldn't tell anyone about the relationship, I had to teach myself how to be the "other woman." I would watch soap operas like "All My Children" to get tips on pleasing "my man." I saw how Erica Kane behaved to get what she wanted, and I even tried to emulate her. I studied and adopted her walk, her behavior, and her tantrums—all to please James.

I became a possessive mess—I experienced fits of rage, jealousy, and envy, and I often had temper tantrums for no apparent reason. I obsessed about other women who I felt were disrespecting James' and my relationship. See, there were other women in our church who were also attracted to James, and I knew it. I was jealous of them because 1) I was a child, and 2) they had an upper hand on me when it came to relationships. I would throw fits, stomp out of the church, and roll my eyes at these women because he was "mine." The seeds of twisted thinking that had been planted had begun sprouting, and new issues that I would battle for the rest of my life were being sown daily.

As the relationship continued, I became the most disliked young lady in the church. Many thought I simply had a bad attitude, while others attributed my behavior to my environment—but I knew the real truth: I was jealous and possessive. I would angrily confront James about these women, but he'd always smile and say that there was nothing going on. He reassured me by telling me that because he was a deacon, he had to be nice to everyone. While I under-stood this, I still battled my own insecurities. *How would this affect me later in life? Will I always be the other woman, battling these insecurities, or is this just a phase that I'll outgrow?* At the time, I wasn't sure; but one thing I now know: I was headed for something that I was not ready for.

CHAPTER THREE

The Innocence Is Lost

No one knew my little secret, and I liked it that way. I'd begun to believe that the reason James wanted our relationship to be kept a secret was because I was so important to him. After all (just like he'd told me), no one would understand "our love." *But was this really love or was it perversion?* You might ask, "How could a forty-two-year-old man claim to be in love with a twelve-year-old child?" Well in my childish eyes, it was because I'd already become a woman—I was nearly thirteen! I thought that perhaps James and I would run away together and start our own family. I didn't realize just how twisted my thoughts were or how obsessed with this man I had become.

James was my mother's favorite nephew, and in her eyes, he could do no wrong. The two of them were in many church ministries together, and I found myself desiring to attend their prayer meetings just to see him. My mother interpreted my actions as a desire to get closer to God. Well, I wanted to get close alright, but not to God. The idea of seeing James, giving him a hug, or having him wink at me from across the room, would satisfy me until the next time we were able to spend time alone together. I wasn't aware of it, but my mind had totally misconstrued the meaning of love. I told myself that I was mature enough to handle anything James desired for us, but in the back of my mind I wondered just how far he would take this relationship.

In August 1977, I turned thirteen, and I felt as if I could conquer the world. Not only was the relationship between James and me getting stronger, but I was also becoming closer to his family and had become like a daughter to him. My mother was so grateful because she saw him as an ideal father figure for me. She was a widow, trying to raise her children on a meager income. I'm quite sure she had financial frustrations; being a single mother was probably overwhelming for her. So it is likely that, in her eyes, help from this strong male would be a definite plus for our family. Besides, my behavior seemed to be improving. My mother must have thought he was doing a great job of being the Godly example that I needed. Little did she know, James and I were headed down a disastrous road.

HAPPY ANNIVERSARY

As time passed, I saw our relationship grow stronger. Before I knew it, we had been secretly seeing each other for a year. I was so happy, because I felt that maybe I was doing something right by giving him what he wanted. As we approached our "anniversary," James began talking about taking our relationship to the next level. I didn't fully understand, so he told me that as my father figure, it was his job to teach me about sex. After all, many fathers taught their children about sex. I figured he would simply take me to the library to research the information, because surely we did not discuss this matter in church. There were no "youth conferences" that allowed us to deal with real issues. We rebuked everything that wasn't Godly and kept shouting in ignorance, while young girls continued having babies out of wedlock.

I wasn't really sure what James had in mind, but I'd become worried that he was planning something that I was not ready for. This didn't stop me, however. I continued fantasizing about him and began writing him love letters. In one particular letter, I expressed my undying love for him, and I told him how much I was looking forward to many more years with him. I gave him the letter at church, as I'd always done, hoping he would take time to write me back. He often took my letters to work and read them during his lunch break, and on a few occasions he actually wrote back to say how much he enjoyed the relationship and to tell me how he felt about me.

But this particular letter, unlike the others, got into the wrong hands. One Saturday morning his wife called to inform me that she'd found the letter in his pocket while washing his clothes. She told me that she was so hurt because all this time she'd been defending this "father/daughter relationship" to the people at church. I was a little shocked. I hadn't realized that people had begun to notice that there was something "strange" about the relationship between James and me. Despite the talk, she'd stood by us, only to learn that the gossipers were right: she was married to a pedophile. At that point, she told me that if I stayed away from him, she would not tell my mother. *What a relief,* I thought. I called James at work to inform him of the phone call, and he was very nonchalant about everything. He told me to call her back and make her believe that it was all my fault and that nothing was going on. Because he assured me that we would be able to continue seeing one another, I called and made her believe that I was a sadistic teenager with problems. It worked, because word never got to my mother, and he never stopped pursuing me.

I'd lied and cheated a lot up until this point in the relationship; I did whatever I thought was necessary so that I could stay with James. I figured that since his wife now knew what was going on, he would end things. But to him, her knowledge of our relationship was not an issue; in fact, he had something more in mind. He tried for months to convince me that it was time to move the relationship forward. Honestly, I was okay with the relationship as it was, but for some reason he desired more. He explained that he wanted us to become physically intimate, and provided me with information about the various types of birth control. He told me that once we took this step, I was only to be sexually active with him until I married. My biggest fear was getting pregnant, having had the negative aspects of such drilled in my head by my mother when we had "the mother-daughter talk." My mother had taught against birth control, because, as she told me, pregnancy was God's way of punishing unmarried girls for fornicating. So I was terrified of becoming pregnant, but I wanted to take the risk for James. Whenever we would meet, the topic would come up. Eventually, I became overwhelmed. James, a typically mild-mannered man, became more and more manipulative. He told me repeatedly that I was the one he wanted and needed to be with. After all, he'd said, he was filling a void in me that I didn't realize was there. *How could I pass up such an opportunity?* So, after months of convincing, I agreed to our first intimate rendezvous. It would take place on a Wednesday night in January 1979.

HE DIDN'T PREPARE ME FOR THIS

The day that James and I were to become intimate, I had mixed emotions. After all, I was only fourteen years old. I was looking forward to seeing him that night, but I was afraid of "the next level." *What would happen if I became pregnant? Was this how I was supposed to lose my virginity? Was this something I really wanted to do, or was I being coerced?* When he arrived to pick me up, he asked my mother if I could go with him to an employee's house and she consented. I loved James, but I was terrified. I knew that I was not ready for this step in our relationship. He had made the necessary motel reservations, and the night was planned. As we drove to the motel, I knew that my life was about to change. We arrived at our destination, and as he went to retrieve the key, a part of me knew that what we were about to do was wrong on many levels. But the perverted part of me wanted to be with my lover. I wanted to experience what I'd heard other girls discuss.

After preparing me for the night and trying to make me feel comfortable, he introduced me to something else I wasn't ready for: child pornography. It terrified me. I was a full-figured girl, ashamed to remove my clothing in front of anyone, including James. Furthermore Gary, "my boogie man," had made me self-conscious about my body. This made me feel even worse. I was with a man who said he loved me, but I didn't feel loved. In fact, I felt sick and I wanted to get out of there. But again, the manipulator played his role brilliantly, convincing me that everything was ok and the plan was back in action. He told me that if I loved him, I would please him. He promised to be gentle with me, and told me that it would not hurt. I thought, *If we are only going to make love, why does he need to take pictures?* I didn't understand the purpose of such photographs—I was afraid he would use them against me later. I felt so dirty and worthless, and when I think of it now, I realize that it was the first time I felt like less than a person. It was so degrading, but he convinced me that this was all part of proving my love for him. Posing for pictures and pleasing my man was no longer what I desired. It wasn't worth it. I felt sick to my stomach, and I told James that I wanted to go home.

When he thought about the money he'd spent on the room, the time he'd put into planning the night, and the fact his sick desire to sleep with a child might not be fulfilled, he was not eager to fulfill my requests to leave. Again, as a master manipulator, he tried to make everything okay. *How was it that he had a wife, but needed me? Was I that special?* Well after about fifteen minutes of convincing me that what he wanted to do was okay, at the tender age of fourteen, I lost my virginity to my forty-four-year-old cousin. My virtue—something that I now know was a gift from God—was gone. This special thing that should have remained with me until I married and entered into a holy covenant had been taken in a perverted and ungodly act, and I could never get it back.

THE DAY AFTER

The ride home was long. I felt so dirty inside, and I wanted to cry. *How could he hurt me like this; how could he say he enjoyed it when I'd bled as if I'd been stabbed? How could he enjoy something that had caused me so much pain?* I knew my life would never be the same, I was physically hurting and didn't know if I needed to tell my mother or not. Maybe there was some internal damage present that I was not aware of. I remember how he'd held my hand and told me that I'd handled myself well. He told me that the more we were intimate, the easier it would be. I sat on the passenger's side of the car, and didn't say a word. I remember thinking to myself, *I never want to do that again; it was too painful.*

We arrived at my house and my mother could tell that something was wrong. She gave me that "What's wrong?" look, and I told her I was tired and that I wanted to go to bed. I remember curling up in bed, crying and holding on to my doll baby, and regretting every-thing I'd done. *Who could I tell, who would believe me, and how could something that's supposed to be beautiful feel so awful?* I got up the next morning and I was unable to bathe myself because of the pain. *Oh my God, why did I hurt so much?* For the first time, I looked in the mirror and saw the fourteen-year-old with pimples and ponytails—the thumb-sucker and bed-wetter—and I asked myself, *"What does he want with me?"*

I had a hard time focusing in school that day, and I kept thinking that I might be pregnant. *What would I tell my mother? How would the people at church look at me? Why was I not happy about what I'd done?* I had so many questions, but no answers. That following Sunday, I sat in my usual seat. But this time, I didn't want to look at James because I felt so ashamed. My entire church routine was disrupted. It had been a ritual for me to leave Sunday school, stand outside, and wait for him and his family to arrive. I'd take the youngest child in my arms and proceed to my seat. This Sunday was different, because I wanted no part of any of them. What seemed strange to me was that I thought I still loved him; I even tried to convince myself that he loved me too. For weeks I regretted what had happened between us, but I was afraid to say how I really felt. I was scared he might leave me and get with another woman in the church (and believe me, there were many waiting in line). I had more questions than ever: *Could I continue this lifestyle? Did I want to continue it? Where was this relationship going and how long would it last?* I felt totally lost, because I knew that he'd taken something away from me that I could never regain: my innocence.

CHAPTER FOUR

Who Will Deliver Me From This Bondage?

After weeks of hearing how beautiful I was, how I made him feel, and how I'd made the right decision, I thought, *Maybe this wasn't so bad after all*. As I now study the minds pedophiles, I've learned that one of their character traits is to twist the truth in an effort to ease the guilt of their own consciences. This was an area that James had mastered with me. He knew what to say, how to say it, and how to smile so that I would believe that our relationship was destined. According to him, because he was older and much wiser, he knew what was best for the both of us. He claimed that he loved me so much that even after his wife learned of our relationship he wanted to continue seeing me. Now that's true love, isn't it? When I think back through the eyes of the adult I've become, I realize that he said these things out of selfishness and nothing else. To convince a child that she's "the woman" meant for an adult man is sadistic and unfair. I did not know that to lose something as precious as my virginity at such a young age would take a lifetime of healing, so I made the decision to stay with him. He was my first boyfriend, and I trusted that we'd be together for ever.

"Lest satan should get an advantage of us: for we are not igno-rant of his devices."
II Corinthians 2:11 (KJV)

In this passage of scripture, the Apostle Paul is warning the church of Corinth that it is well aware of the devices of satan; therefore, the enemy should be unable to take advantage of the church. Well, like many young believers, I was ignorant of the devices of the enemy. I never saw the devil's tactics in my relationship with James. My struggles with low self-esteem, the loss of my self respect, and the taking of my innocence never occurred to me to be tactics that the devil was using in an attempt to destroy me. I saw myself as a young girl who was lucky because this handsome man, whom many desired, had chosen me. If that wasn't deception, I don't know what is.

Although I was forbidden to tell anyone about the relationship and was definitely forbidden to have a boyfriend, it was still fine with me to maintain "the secret." I felt like I had the best of everything: a mature man who loved me, who cared for me, and who was careful to ensure that I did not get pregnant. Since getting pregnant was like an epidemic in my neighborhood, I felt special because I knew I could have sex and not have anything to worry about. When I think of it now, it wasn't so much that he cared for or even loved me. Basically, I fulfilled a sick desire he had for children. He knew that if I became pregnant, he would lose everything and would probably be imprisoned. So he continued saying what I needed to hear, convincing me how beautiful I was—even telling me I was more beautiful than his wife. It was like a fairy tale to me, this man loved me more than he loved his wife—so he said.

How long could I keep this secret? Writing love letters, talking on the phone, and receiving the ungodly hugs in church were getting old and stale. I wondered if it would always be this way or if things would change for us. As he continued to convince me of his undying love—which was a lie—he would coach me about which lies to tell my mother so that we could continue to see each other. I never thought twice about the lies I told her; I just wanted to see him. I even knew that being with him again would mean another evening of degrading myself, but I didn't care. I just wanted to be with him. I was involved in something that I didn't understand and had no idea how to get out of.

A NEW RENDEVOUS

When I lost my virginity, I was fourteen years old. I had been introduced to sex quite early and now I was craving it. It was not that I was craving a desire to be with James again but I had become one with him through sexual intimacy. Paul says in I Corinthians 6:16 (KJV) *"What? know ye not that he which is joined to an harlot is one body? for the two, saith he, shall be one flesh."* One important thing many single individuals fail to realize is that when sex is practiced outside of marriage, it causes an ungodly transfer of spirits. This is why the scripture says, "...the two shall become one," meaning that when a man and woman become married and they consummate that marriage, they become one. Many of us have engaged in sexual relations with so many men that we have joined with everybody except the one God ordained. I thought I desired James because I was in love, but the reality was, I had become familiar with an unclean spirit, and I desired to fill that lustful need. Because of my experiences with him, I not only desired to be around James, but I also found myself wanting to fulfill my own sexual desires. I regularly practiced self-gratification, and my desire became very intense. I had become like a predator after its prey—searching, looking, and waiting for the opportunity to pounce. The spirit of perversion had found me. I didn't care where I was, what time of day or night it was, or where we met, I just wanted him. For me, it was no longer about being in love; it was now about being satisfied. *How could I have become so perverted at such a young age?*

During this era, our church lacked the resources to hire individuals in ministry, so many people volunteered their services. There were no full-time secretaries, pastors, custodians, or musicians. We would give love offerings followed by the familiar line, "We're not trying to pay you, but your reward is in heaven." Well if you heard that, you could rest assured that you were getting no more than ten dollars. Regardless, we were grateful to receive it. James was the church clerk, the pastor's right-hand man, and the custodian. Many times he would ask my mother if I could come over to the church to help him clean. To her, this was one sure way that I had something to do on Saturdays. So of course my mother released me into the hands of this "Godly" man, to clean up our place of worship.

Well, church became the new meeting place for James and me. The first time we were together there, he let me know that we were safe and that it was okay for us to meet there. He also told me that he was probably the only one who had a key, and that he was definitely the only one to come to the church on Saturday. So there I was—in the sanctuary with this married, adult man holding me in his arms. A red flag went up: *this is not right, we are in church.* No, he told me, we're going in the Sunday school room, which is not the sanctuary, it's just a classroom. Again, thinking that he's much wiser and more mature, I agreed. He explained that the sanctuary was sacred but the Sunday school classrooms were different and that I should trust him. Eventually, he convinced me that being together in the classrooms was okay.

Eventually, our new meeting place became okay with me, although I still had a slight feeling that it was not right. James continued to tell me that it didn't matter that we met in church, because this was the only way we could continue seeing each other. The fact that I'd agreed at that point showed my disrespect and lack of reverence for the house of God. Just like our meeting place had changed, I had also changed. My language had become very vulgar, and my letters were no longer sweet and innocent. Instead, I began using the language of an adult woman. It didn't seem to bother James at all. After all, his desires were being fulfilled.

The more we met, the more I wanted to meet. I no longer cared about the morals, values, or Christian teachings concerning our relationship. He'd convinced me that he was not committing adultery, because we were "kissing cousins," and there was nothing wrong with that. I figured that he should know, but the truth was, I knew as well. Relatives who kissed in a romantic way were doing something wrong, and I knew it. But I was so deep into this relationship that I didn't care. I had literally trained myself to believe this was the life I desired, that this was the man for me, and that God would make it work. But in the back of my mind I knew I was wrong and that I was stuck.

I began to be overtaken by fear. We would have "tarrying services" on Friday nights, and there were some powerful women of God who seemed to have an ability to "see" everything. I witnessed these women cast out demons and prophesy to people until they confessed, so I was always afraid they would see what was going on with me. *Did God love me so much that he wouldn't expose me?* When I think of it now, I know that it would have done more damage for this "secret" to have been exposed; therefore God had mercy on us. The many times we met, we were never caught. We were not lucky; we were under the mercy of God.

LET A MAN EXAMINE HIMSELF

"So anyone who eats this bread or drinks this cup of the Lord unworthily is guilty of sinning against the body and the blood of the Lord. That is why you should examine yourself before eating the bread and drinking from the cup. For if you eat the bread or drink the cup without honoring the body of Christ, you are eating and drinking God's judgment upon yourself."
I Corinthians 11:27–29 (NLT)

As I now teach New Discipleship Training at my church, I often teach the Lord's Supper as a sacrament of the church. I stress how important it is for us to examine ourselves that we don't drink or eat unworthily. It is a dangerous thing to be a part of the body of Christ and not care about how you represent yourself as a believer. In this passage, Paul tells the people of the church of Corinth that they should take the Lord's Supper—or as we call it, Communion— very seriously. How many times have believers taken the Lord's Supper with no regard to the unforgiveness in their hearts or the bitterness they hold against their spouses, supervisors, or their next-door neighbors?

I remember the many times we had Communion services; it was always on the third Sunday and produced a full house. The chairman of our deacon board would always read this scripture, and many of the kids became afraid, because we knew we had committed some type of sin. The choir would gently sing "He Was Nailed to the

Cross," and the pastor would elaborate on the importance of the service. I would watch my mother and other members cry and lift their hands to worship and thank God. I never really understood all of the emotions at the time, but I do now that I'm older, and I understand Calvary. During these services, James was often asked to pray over the communion, asking God to change it from "a natural to a spiritual" substance. Many times I wondered how he could pray with such passion, knowing he was married and having a relationship with me.

As a minister today, I understand this mindset a little better. Whenever we practice sin, we allow room for the enemy to justify to us that we're right. Although we know the truth or have been convicted by the Spirit, when it comes to pleasing the flesh, there is always a battle. I don't believe that neither James nor I had allowed ourselves to become fully aware of our sinful ways, because we always justified our love for each other. The more we came together and the more we talked, I believe we convinced each other that the relationship was ordained. By the time I was approaching fifteen, I no longer gave a second thought to my actions. I had become very promiscuous, and I attributed that to the fact that I had been with an older man. I had gotten to the point that I not only wanted James to give me attention, but also I began longing for attention from other older men. In my mind I had become the woman that every man desired. I was very flirtatious, frisky, and bold in my actions.

As time went on, I became more desperate and wanted to take more risks. I had stopped caring about where James and I met. I would talk about other men or boys from school to make him jealous. I didn't understand that pretending to be one of the soap opera stars would not work in reality. My attitude changed—I tried to change the way I dressed because I needed James to know that I was the sultry woman he needed me to be. My mind was twisted, and I was spiritually entangled in something that would take me at least ten years to be delivered from. My boldness began to scare James, but I was just acting the way I thought I should in order to keep the man I believed was destined for me. What deception!

WHO WILL DELIVER ME FROM THIS MESS?

"O wretched man that I am! who shall deliver me from the body of this death?"
Romans 7:24 (KJV)

I fully understand the dilemma the Apostle Paul faced: wanting to do right, knowing you should do right, but doing wrong instead. One of my favorite gospel singers is Pastor Hezekiah Walker. He wrote a song several years ago entitled, "You're calling my name." Before the choir sings, he ministers with some thought-provoking questions: "How many times have you been doing the wrong thing, and you knew that it was wrong?" I knew that what I was doing with James was totally out of the will of God for me, but I continued on.

I struggled with thoughts of doing the right thing versus staying with the man I loved, and at the age of sixteen, I decided to stay with James. I was at my mother's "legal age" of dating, but James had forbidden any other man to come into my life. He said I should save myself for my husband and if I dated, there was a possibility that I would become sexually active and get pregnant. I tried to convince him that I loved him and would not cheat on him, but he didn't agree. What I understand now is that I'd been introduced to sex and I was craving it; therefore, he knew that regardless of whether I loved him, if the desire was strong enough, I would yield. So it was best for him to dissuade me from dating rather than take that chance. While others were attending the prom, not only did my mother's Christian beliefs dictate that the prom was not for saved girls, but James also convinced me that I didn't need to go. Furthermore, the suspicion of our relationship was spreading further than our church, and James had to make some drastic changes. Our small congregation was not only becoming suspicious, but people outside of our church were also watching. We could no longer walk in ignorance, believing we were right. The scripture is true, *"There is a way which seemeth right unto a man, but the end thereof are the ways of death,"* (Proverbs 14:12 [KJV]). I could no longer blame James for my participation in this ungodly relationship. I'd heard enough sermons, and knew enough of God's Word to know that my actions were wrong. I knew things had to change, but I was in such a mess that I didn't know what to do.

In the past, it had been common for me to ride to church with James, but that was coming to a halt. People were speculating that something was wrong with our relationship. What puzzled me, though, was that I was the one being blamed for the relationship. Whenever the rumors circulated, I was named as the culprit, and James idly stood by and said nothing in my defense. I was now experiencing rejection from James. For years he'd told me he loved me, but now the story was changing. I would cry when he refused to meet me after church, and I felt neglected when he walked down the other aisle of the church as he ignored me. I couldn't understand why things were different, until he explained that he still wanted to be with me — he just had to be careful. To me, however, it seemed as if he only wanted me when it was convenient for him.

GOD CAN DELIVER

Soon everything began falling apart around me. The phone calls ceased, as did the "I love you" speeches, and while I was hurting, I realized that I was involved in something that God didn't desire for my life. I approached James one night after a powerful revival, where for the first time, I'd experienced a strong Godly conviction. I cried out to God that night at the altar, begging and pleading with Him to help me change. I really didn't understand what I needed, and I didn't trust anyone enough to share the reason for my weeping. All I knew was that I was tired of this mess. I knew that there was a call on my life, but I wasn't strong enough spiritually to walk away from what I had with James. He'd witnessed the entire altar experience, and the next night at the revival we chatted, and he smartly stated, "I guess now you want to go straight and leave me." The spirit of manipulation was at work again. So I suggested that we stop being intimate but continue to see each other. He agreed, but that didn't last long. As I look at it now, I really believe I was in the beginning stages of my deliverance. While I felt it was impossible to change or be free from this bondage, God had begun to show me that he could deliver. We were no longer seeing each other as frequently as we had been, but we were still entangled in sin. I no longer had the excuse: "I'm a child," because although I was still a minor, I knew better. Not only that but I had now experienced a move of God in my life enough to know that I could be delivered.

The guilt was wearing on me because I was being introduced to good preaching and teaching. I remember having a restless week and coming under conviction by the Holy Spirit. I thought that if I changed my hair, bought a new dress, and put on a little makeup, it would change the way that I felt inside, but that was to no avail. I felt like I was in a hole and couldn't get out. I tried to ignore the feeling, I tried to run from it, and I even pretended that I didn't understand it. But I knew that the Spirit was tugging at my heart to trust Him and walk away from James. I just didn't know how to take the first step. I wondered as the Apostle Paul did in Romans chapter seven, *"Who will free me from this life that is dominated by sin?"* I needed someone to talk to, but who could I trust? At the same time, who would believe that James was molesting *me*? No one would—they all thought it was my fault. So I figured that this was something I just had to get through alone. I remember the comments of many of the church members and the way they judged me. They would often say, "You should be ashamed of yourself, having a crush on your cousin, he's a married man." Instead of seeing that I was being abused sexually, they looked at me like I was a stalker. So while I wanted to change and I wanted to get out of the mess I was in, no one was willing to help me. No one saw that I needed help or even heard my cries for help. I continued living with this deep, dark secret, desiring to change but unable to. When I would share with James the desire to be free, there was such a stronghold of manipulation working that I walked away feeling defeated. *Who would deliver me from this bondage?*

CHAPTER FIVE

Same Spirit, Different Man

I am thoroughly convinced that the old adage is true: "If you play with fire, you will get burned." In other words, you can't sit under good biblical teaching, understand the Word, and not see a need for change. If you hang around the Word long enough, the fire of God will eventually expose the sin in your life. You can't experience the love and mercy of God without applying it to your life sooner or later.

> *"Seek ye the LORD while He may be found, call ye upon Him while He is near:"*
> **Isaiah 55:6 (KJV)**

While I was still a victim of incest, I would often pray and ask God to help me become a better person. What I didn't realize was that although my prayers were coming out of my mouth, God was really hearing my heart. I never asked God to take me out of the relationship with James, but when the Holy Spirit made intercession for me, I'm quite sure that's how my prayers were delivered. I would always pray that God would help me to be a better person, because I was so insecure, mean, and rebellious. Although these characteristics stemmed from the years of sexual abuse, I didn't want to remain in this state. I didn't have friends, because I had been labeled as a trouble-maker Therefore, I had no one to confide in and no one who understood *why* I acted the way I did. During the many times that I was called to the altar, oiled down, and prayed for, the only thing I was ever told was that I had a spirit of rebellion. *Couldn't anyone see what was really going on with me?* I wasn't mean because I wanted to be. I was lashing out and looking for help. Although my prayer life was not mature, I had learned one thing from my Aunt Magdalene: if you call on Jesus, He will answer your prayer. So as I continued praying, "Lord help me to be a better person," I was seeking the Lord and calling upon His name. I was looking for God to change me without actually saying those words. To be honest, I didn't know how to seek God without a lot of ritual and religious theatrics. But I knew I wanted to change.

I had become affiliated with some new churches whose pastors really taught the Word. They were calling sin what it was, no holds barred. I had been in the ministry of music since the age of thirteen and had begun to affiliate with new young people who were really serious about God. Most Sundays, I didn't attend my church; I attended with my new friends at theirs. I would see the power of God move on them like nothing else I'd ever seen, and I desired to be in a relationship with God so that I could experience that same power. But, because I was so rebellious, it was hard for me to surrender and allow the power of God to consume me. I had to be in control, because I wasn't sure what God would do to me, and I was not willing to take such a risk. In my mind, if I surrendered, I might be hurt again, and I was not up for anymore pain. I'd lost my trust in everyone, because it seemed that those who had been called to watch over me had abused me. I felt I couldn't trust God either. I was convinced—no one else would ever have that type of control over me again. Thus, I often left services feeling empty and thinking that God didn't love me like He loved my friends. What I didn't know was that they had surrendered—something I'd refused to do. The good thing is that it didn't change the way I prayed: *God help me to be a better person. God help me to be happy for others when they succeed; help me not to be jealous of someone who looks better than me or who accomplished a goal that I only dreamed of accomplishing.*

While I was being transformed, I still had some contact with James. We didn't see each other as much though, so things were really cooling down between us. The attraction and desire I'd had for him was slowly, but surely, leaving me. I realized how sick and sadistic the relationship had been and I desired to seek after God. I had become a little stronger in the faith, and I began applying the Word to my situation. In addition, I was becoming older and preparing to graduate from high school. James knew I was no longer the little girl he once manipulated and controlled. He no longer tried to convince me that what he'd done was okay. I guess he had conquered what he'd sought out to conquer, and the thrill for him was gone. I was no longer the sweet, innocent child; I was moving into adulthood and was no longer a "chase" for him. We would talk frequently, but we never talked about the relationship. We acted as though it had never happened. I believe we both wanted to pretend that it had been a bad dream, but we both knew that it hadn't been. One day we would have to deal with what we'd done.

IT'S FINALLY OVER

By 1982, I had graduated from high school and was preparing to attend Norfolk State University. I'd planned to join as many activities as I could to consume my thoughts, so that I could forget the terrible things that had happened in my life. I wanted to forget the molestation, the lesbianism, and the incest. I taught myself to believe: *if you don't think about it, then it won't be true.* What a myth! As I began my freshman year at college, I encountered a lot of things and was introduced to many people. I figured I could handle it; after all, I had survived years of worse. What I didn't understand was the toll the abuse had taken on me emotionally. I also didn't realize that the spirit of perversion was still upon me—dormant—to make me believe I was okay. I thought a couple of emotional "hallelujah times" in church constituted healing, when in fact, it only meant the Spirit passed through, and I had surrendered at that moment. Although I was feeling mature on the outside, I still had the mind of a child when it came to my emotions, my insecurities, and the plan of God for my life. I was clueless. By this time, James and I had little to no contact, because I was ready to date openly. I wanted someone to take me to the movies, out to dinner, or to just hang out with me, and what I'd had with James was no longer fulfilling or desired.

My mother had always taught me to work for what you want. So I had been working in the ministry of music since age thirteen and working as a student aide with the U.S. government since age sixteen. After I was in college for a year, I purchased my first vehicle and began looking to move out on my own. The great thing was that I was moving out alone. As I prepared for adulthood, my dealings with James were coming to an end. I learned that someone else found me attractive—someone who was not married, whom I could be seen with in public, and whom I could share with my family. I felt free—I could finally date.

I met Dwayne during the winter semester at Norfolk State. I was so excited because I was finally dating someone and I didn't have to hide it. It was close to Christmas and we were preparing to leave for the holidays. I had been talking to Dwayne for about three weeks, and he invited me over to his home for a big Christmas party. The house was decorated so beautifully; it made me feel like Cinderella. We decided to stay for a while before leaving to meet some of Dwayne's friends for another little party. As we approached the apartment, I noticed it was dark. I became suspicious, but he told me that his friends had gone out and left him with the key. Now, I'd believed many lies in the past, but this one nearly cost me my life. Dwayne's friends were out of town and had asked him to watch their place while they were away. His intention was to be intimate with me, and I was clueless.

While we waited for his friends to return, which never happened, we began to fool around with each other. I didn't want to take things too far, which irritated him to the point of violence. Dwayne raped me and threatened to kill me. I remember being slammed into a wall with his hand around my throat. The sweet young man, whom I had trusted, had become a different person when I told him no. Full of fear, I thought I would never see my mother again, and because she knew nothing of Dwayne, there was nothing she'd be able to tell the police. I had told her another one of my "church lies" to get out of the house. I had been so accustomed to lying that this time I'd lied without cause. As the violence continued, I just stopped fighting and surrendered. I figured it would be over soon, and maybe I could get over this trauma, too. I prayed, "God if you would get me out of this, I'll never tell my mother another lie." After it was over, I escaped never to see him again. I wanted to tell someone what had happened to me, but instantly I thought, "Who will believe me?" We all know that date rape is hard to prove. So, I chose to live with yet another secret and tried to move on with my life. I figured it would be another trophy in my "abuse cabinet."

I returned home that night feeling like my life was just one big story of abuse. From age five until age nineteen, my life had been filled with men who had taken advantage of me and used my body for their own sexual pleasure. Despite dating Dwayne for a short time, I was still somewhat involved with James. But at this point, I wanted nothing to do with any of them. I just wanted to be loved, respected, and understood. The problem with this was that I didn't love, respect, or understand myself; therefore, I didn't know what to demand from others.

I continued working at the Naval Shipyard and pursuing my college degree. Although it wasn't officially over, James would call every once in a while to see how I was doing. One particular day he said, "I want to talk to you when you get a chance." I knew where his conversation was going. After all, it had been at least a year and a half since we had been intimate or had paid any real attention to each other. We casually talked from time to time and had passed each other in church, but our relationship had basically ended with neither of us saying a word. Not wanting to wait for a meeting, I suggested that we talk right away. He said, "I want to go straight, I don't want to do this anymore." I politely agreed and hung up. Finally, it was over. The little giggly girl with the ponytails, who was wetting the bed and sucking her thumb, was no longer available to thrill him. We no longer had a connection to one another, nor were we attracted to each other. I was finally out of that God-forbidden relationship, and I finally felt free.

A NEW GAME TO PLAY

It was all over; the church people had either stopped talking or were at least talking less. I felt as if I were a free bird and on my way to a better life. However, all of that changed when the seeds of perversion began to sprout and take over my life. I was continuing my college education, affiliating with other churches, and making new friends, all while enjoying the attention I received from the men at these churches. The first time I was approached by a young man, he too was married. While I knew it was wrong, I was very comfortable with this type of relationship. After all, I had failed with single men and married men alike, so what difference did it make? This new man told me how unhappy he was and that his life was miserable. He said he loved his wife, but she had become boring and he wanted more in a relationship. Something inside of me said, "You're the one he needs."

I didn't understand that a spirit was working in me, and, because I'd listened to the enemy so much, I was easily deceived into believing that I "had it going on like that." I took pride in my beauty, my feminine wiles, and what I felt I could do to keep a man. My motto was, "What his wife won't do, I will." To make sure that I had the "upper hand" in the bedroom, I had also begun to engage in pornography. I would often borrow tapes from my "sailor friends" in an effort to educate myself. While I saw many of the acts on these tapes as unthinkable, I also knew many of these things were not happening in marriage. Therefore, I figured that my motto was on point. In addition, I began using my music ministry as a way of getting men; the enemy used me as one of his tools to break up marriages. I would often play at churches and scope out the weak-willed men in the church. Because I had plenty of experience in conniving to get what I wanted, I often knew what to say and how to say it. While I thought I was a fine "red bone," I failed to understand that the enemy had a resting place in my mind and that he was using me to destroy the thing God loved: oneness. I didn't care how long the couple had been married, whether I knew them, or if I was close with the family. If I saw a man I wanted, I went after him. *What has happened to me and why was I acting in this manner?*

I was playing a new game. Instead of being pursued, manipulated, controlled, and abused, I was now manipulating and controlling to get what I wanted. I was determined: no longer would a man have control over me or touch me in a manner that degraded me. I was in charge, and I was calling all of the shots. I was very strategic in my attack to get a man. If he had children, I befriended them first, and then I would befriend the wife. Often, I'd pay her compliments, telling her whatever lies I felt were necessary to win her over. Once I won the family's confidence, I would be introduced to the man, but I'd pretend that he wasn't important. After I made sure that I was "in good" with the family, I'd hook my claws in him and wreak havoc in the home.

As I transferred to different churches, serving as the minister of music, the game became more exciting to me. I never cared about the marriage that I destroyed, or the wife who trusted me as a friend, only to realize she'd been betrayed. You see, I'd learned how to play at an early age; it came natural to me. I only cared about being satisfied. I was like a cougar in the woods, watching the prey, and when the time was right, I would attack. I had a destructive spirit that was attached to revenge. As I understand it now, I was on an assignment to destroy as many men as I could because of the abuse I'd suffered. I had become skilled at what I did, and if things looked as if they were getting out of hand or if it seemed that someone would find out, I simply moved on to my next demonic assignment. I did not want a relationship; I only wanted a thrill. I didn't want love, either. All I wanted was the fulfillment of my perverted desires.

Where was this behavior coming from? How did I learn to be so cunning and devious while working in ministry? While desiring to get over the years I'd been involved with my cousin James and acquaint myself with new spirit-filled friends, somehow I'd missed what was most important—developing relationship with God. While my mind desired this, my body desired something else. I found myself going from church to church, scoping out men who were having marital problems. I no longer cared about the ministry of music; I felt as if I were getting revenge on all the men who'd hurt me. *Will life be different for me or will I always battle promiscuity?* Although I'd stopped seeing James, his impartation of sexual sin was still in me.

I had become familiar with using my body for favors or being the other woman. Basically, the same spirit was in me; I'd simply found a different man.

What spirit had I encountered that caused me to act in this manner? I had become no better than the prostitute on the street. Was my behavior a result of my belief that I could attract any man I wanted, or had a spirit been transferred to me? Because I am more knowledgeable now of the dangers of premarital sex, I am fully aware that there were many ungodly spirits transferred to me. That's why the Bible specifically says "flee fornication." That means run from it; get away from it. Many single individuals don't understand that every time they sleep with someone, there is a transferring of spirits. It's not that the intimate moment was so great that it causes you to want more; rather, the spirit in each of them is now calling after its own kind. I know now that my influence had nothing to do with my beauty, my figure, or anything else. It was the spirit of lust. While I made myself believe that I was getting revenge, I had only switched roles. I was now the manipulator and the controller—I had the upper hand.

CHAPTER SIX

The Spirit of the Concubine

"If the Son therefore shall make you free, ye shall be free indeed."
John 8:36 (KJV)

Growing up in the Pentecostal denomination, I saw a lot of things I understood and some things I questioned. Even today, at the age of forty-three, I still have questions about some of the routines of the worship service. If the mothers of the church knew someone was struggling with a particular sin or if they heard a person was, they were eager to get that person "delivered." They often called the individual and his or her sin to the front—which was quite embarrassing, I'm sure—but declaring that the person needed to be free. Many times we went to the altar voluntarily to avoid the public embarrassment. Once at the altar, we were instructed about how to receive deliverance: we repeated, "Jesus" over and over, faster and faster, while one of the church mothers would stand over us saying, "Yeah, yeah, that's it, you've got it, you've got it, there it is..." Many times I walked away wondering, what do I have, what did I get, and why do I feel the same? The answer: I was not free. I'd only gone through a ritual that somehow older saints believed was required in order for deliverance to take place. While the mothers felt they were doing the right thing, they often moved in error. Therefore, we attended "tarry services" on Friday nights, while others were at football games and school dances. We were always in the prayer line, where someone was there to cast one demon or another out of us; however, we still had a high percentage of teenage pregnancy in our church. Why? Because we were not free.

Some churches have confused "deliverance" with "feeling good for the moment." We've misunderstood an encounter with God for an experience with God. Therefore, we find people coming to the altar in pain and leaving the same way. They cry real tears, but in their hearts they really don't want to totally surrender; perhaps they don't know how to surrender. Some really have a strong desire to change, but as they engage in that "old ritual" of tarrying, they find themselves right back in the same place. They are likely praying the same prayer I had, "Lord get me out of this," but like me, they somehow found themselves returning to the same situation. I'd told God that I wanted to be loved, but I didn't know what "true love" was. So I continued to seek love in various relationships and continued being "the other woman."

TRADING SINS

"Now ye are clean through the word which I have spoken unto you."
John 15:3 (KJV)

The grave mistake that many people make when walking through deliverance is that they do not allow the Word of God to completely cleanse the residue of pain. Since I was no longer a victim or a participator in an incestuous relationship, I felt that I'd been freed and delivered from what was hurting me inside. I had changed my associations and churches, but that did not bring deliverance. The residue of guilt, shame, and sin were still a part of my life. I had learned to trade sins. While I've never been an alcoholic, I know people who have been. One thing they've shared with me is their struggle with "trading habits"—meaning, they may have stopped drinking, but now they overeat. Some don't do drugs anymore, but now they smoke cigarettes. In my case, I was no longer being sexually abused, but now I was entangled with many sexual demons. Somehow, I'd begun to believe that one of the reasons I was on earth was to satisfy men no matter the cost to my emotional or spiritual self. I didn't care if I knew these men well; I didn't care if they were married or if they had girlfriends. There was a seed that had been planted in me that caused me to trade the destruction placed upon me through sexual abuse for the self-destruction of my own body. I was no longer the little girl who sucked her thumb; I had become the "red bone" who knew how to satisfy her man.

By 1986, I was free from it all—at least I thought I was. I was working a steady job in Portsmouth when I was approached by an older gentleman named Henry. I thought that becoming involved with him would provide me with a way to stop having affairs with the other men I'd been entangled with. This man was charming, handsome, and had a silver tongue. He would say whatever was necessary to get exactly what he wanted. He approached my desk, and we began to talk. We shared lunch together; he'd call to check on me and would often bring me breakfast. I thought I'd finally found a man who would respect and love me. Not only that, but this man could sing like Luther Vandross, and since I was in the ministry of music, he captivated me. We would often have lunch together, talk, and sing old-school songs or hymns. I felt as if I'd found my dream man.

As time went on, this man charmed me; he said what I needed to hear. After all, I was broken, hurt, bruised, and had no idea of who I was. I was looking for someone to validate me, and here he was. Not only could he sing, but he was also a Christian and an ordained minister. I thought, *God must be on my side.* In addition to that, he was being considered for the pastorate at a local church. I figured I could have it all, now. I would sit and daydream about him as pastor and me as the first lady. I thought I'd met Mr. Right. I began dating this man, and we soon became intimate. I knew it was wrong, but he assured me that things would be alright, because we all had struggles; God would still love us. He stood firmly on the scripture that says, *"For the gifts and calling of God are without repentance,"* (Romans 11:29 [KJV]). This was his justification for fornicating even though he was called to preach. He claimed that God would continue to use him regardless of his lifestyle and that repentance was not necessary. He also shared the teaching that "once saved, you're always saved." His explanation was that once we accepted Jesus we have eternal salvation. Regardless of how we lived, what we did, who we cheated, who we slept with, how disobedient we were, it didn't matter—we didn't have to seek forgiveness or repent. Again, once we initially repented, we could live free and wild like the world we were in. Needless to say, I was not the first girlfriend this preacher had lured into fornication using this doctrine. But it didn't see that at the time. I was not taught this concept in my growing up, but somehow it sounded good. It was pleasing to the flesh, so I decided to give it a try. After all, he even had scripture that I thought justified what we did in our relationship. He was much more mature than I was—twenty years my senior—so I knew he could take care of me. I thought I had hit the jack pot. We spent time together: he called, visited, met my mother, and even attended church with me. He would run revivals and my sister and I would provide the music. I thought life was wonderful! While many thought we all were a spiritual team, what they didn't know was that he was my lover, and after he finished preaching, it was off to the races.

Once, Henry didn't come to work for a week, and I wondered what had happened. When he returned, he informed me that his mother-in-law had passed from cancer. Mother-in-law—meaning you are married? He replied to me calmly, "Yes, I thought you knew." I had officially become his concubine. I had spent time with him, I had been intimate with him, I had been seen around town with him, I was allowed to drive his vehicle, and I had fallen in love with him. Ours was no secret relationship. His co-workers and some of his friends knew who I was, so why didn't any of them tell me he was married? *How did this happen? How did I fall into the same trap again?* I had to make a decision whether to stay or leave. I loved him so much and thought I needed him; he made me feel good about myself. What harm could it do? He lived across town so I figured that his wife would never learn of our relationship. I settled for what he offered and thought it was okay. Somehow in my mind, though, I still felt that it was my responsibility to do what his wife wouldn't or couldn't do for him. It was an honor to be this preacher's lover, to support his ministry, to take care of his needs, and be there for him. I was doing it again—repeating what I'd learned from my relationship with my cousin. I knew quite well how to be the other woman; I knew how to tell the right lies and how to sneak around so that I could see him.

My mother loved this man because he was "good" for her baby girl, and he was a minister. She, too, thought I'd hit the jackpot. I continued seeing Henry, knowing he was married. Another cycle was being repeated in my life. I knew the game; I knew the talk; and I was ready to move forward with this man. I became very devious in my actions, sometimes playing games to show him that he would not push me around. He made a mistake, though. He told me that if he received the pastoral position, our relationship was over. But I knew he was not getting rid of me that easily. I decided that it was time for me to design myself a little "insurance."

THE ULTIMATE SCHEME

For years women have thought that if they had a man's baby, he'd stay around. That could not be further from the truth. If a man wants to be with you, he'll stay, and if he doesn't want to be with you, he'll leave. I knew it was possible that Henry could be chosen for the pastorate, because they called him to preach more than any other Pastoral candidate. I loved him, and I thought he loved me. So I figured maybe, just maybe, he'd leave his wife for me. What could I do to keep him and assure that he'd be with me?

The deadline was quickly approaching, and the church was nearly ready to make their decision. He tried to break off the relationship early, and I was heartbroken. I said to him, "We can be friends," and he agreed. Before I knew it, we were seeing each other again. I wanted this man; he gave me a feeling of security when I was with him, and I thought things were okay until he called to tell me that the church had asked him to become their pastor. It was over—I was devastated! I had even prayed that God would somehow keep us together. How absurd! See, when you are in sin, you become blind and ignorant to the ways of God. Why would God work on my behalf to keep this relationship going, when it was definitely outside of His will? I knew I had to do something, so to celebrate his new assignment we had one last night together so that I could implement my scheme, and it worked. I became pregnant.

I really wasn't aware of what was going on, but knew my body was going through some rough changes. I told Henry that I thought I was pregnant, and of course, he was panic-stricken. He denied being the father and didn't want to have anything to do with me anymore. When he began his assignment at the new church, I attended the first service. I wanted to let him know that I would not be pushed aside as if I'd never meant anything to him. I would attend his revivals and other services just to keep him nervous. What scared him most was my association with his wife. He knew I had an aggressive personality, and he was not sure what I would say to her.

As the weeks went by, I began to feel worse and worse, so my mother encouraged me to see my obstetrician. Once there, I learned some painful news: I had miscarried. I would have to have an emergency procedure; the pregnancy was over. I had decided not to tell Henry what happened, because I wanted him to "sweat it out" a little while longer, and it worked. I was wreaking havoc on Henry's life. He never knew when I would show up at his mother's house, because I had made friends with his sisters. He also knew that at any time I could be sitting in front of his house or ringing the door bell. I had become a "fatal attraction," who was becoming more devious by the minute. He began to ignore me at work; he stopped returning my phone calls, and had declared our relationship to be officially over. Eventually, nothing I did moved him; he was going to live the life God had called him to live, and that was it.

Still determined, I did everything in my power to stay with him. He had changed his home number to an unpublished listing, and somehow I found it and begin harassing him again. When he refused to play my childish game, I told him I would tell his church and wife that I was carrying his child. I knew I had him. When he came back to me, I wondered if he'd done it because he loved me or if he'd returned out of fear. Of course, when we got back together, things between us were not the same; you can't force someone to love you, to want to be with you, or to want you to be their lover. When the love is gone, it's over.

I FINALLY GOT IT!

The more I demanded, the more he avoided me. For two years I'd patiently been "the other woman," and now it was coming to an end. *Did he love God more than he loved me? Had the Spirit convicted him, making him realize that God had more for both of us?* This could have been the reason, but I saw it as outright rejection. It made me angry, and I plotted my revenge against him. After several weeks, he found out that I had lied about the pregnancy. It wasn't enough for me to walk away with a little bit of remaining dignity, but I decided to add insult to his injury. When he questioned me about the pregnancy, I rudely replied, "I had an abortion; I'd rather kill your child than have it." How cruel. He was crushed, devastated, and in my sadistic little mind, I really thought he would come running back to me. I had tried everything, and so I finally faced the truth: *he didn't want me anymore.* He was a middle-aged man who'd had a fling and I had been his toy for the moment. It was over.

As I recovered from that disastrous ordeal, I began to look forward to the holidays and the approaching year. My mother's birthday was on Christmas day, and we'd planned a wonderful sixtieth birthday party for her. I found myself wanting Henry to be a part of the celebration because my mother had been very fond of him. He agreed to attend for my mother's sake, and he made it clear that I should not get any other ideas. I took his response for what it was, kept my distance, and enjoyed seeing the excitement on my mother's face as she opened the box containing the diamond ring I'd given her. She looked at me and said, "When I die, don't bury this with me—take it back." I thought, *What an unusual thing to say.* What I didn't know then was that my mother knew she was dying, but hadn't told us because she didn't want us to worry. We ended up having a wonderful Christmas that year, and I came to grips with the fact that it was over between Henry and me. I finally realized that he would never leave his wife for me and if he did, it would only be a matter of time before he left me for someone else—he'd made that clear on more than one occasion. So I decided to move on.

DOOM'S DAY

Thank God for a new year—1988. My mother had been ill, but had started to improve. Despite numerous tests, cardiologists still couldn't determine what was truly going on with her heart. I was so afraid of dealing with my mother's illness; she was the prayer warrior of the family—she really knew God. I only knew of the God she talked about. When she became sick, I remember wondering, *If she dies, who will pray me through my messes? Who will pray me out of what I am dealing with?* Thus, I prayed continuously, "Mother, please get better."

As I faced a life without Henry, I realized that I needed to get rid of everything that reminded me of our relationship. In February of 1988, I tore up every card; I sent every picture back to him; and I wrote him a letter to let him know that I was calling things off for good. See, although he had called it quits, we had still been seeing each other for short rendezvous to satisfy our sinful desires. I was still not his girlfriend, nor was I the other woman. I had simply become a "booty call." I had hit rock bottom. I wanted to be with this man, but he was married; I wanted to walk away, but I was entangled sexually. I desired better, but didn't know what better was. I did know, however, that something had to change. Henry called me when he received the package I'd sent; he knew it was over for good. He told me that he respected me and that he would leave me alone. I had to face doom's day: the relationship with the man I loved was really, officially over.

I kept thinking that life surely had to get better than this—I figured it just had to. I wondered what I could do to make a better life. I only knew "church"; I didn't know *relationship*. I was looking for something, but I didn't know what I was looking for. Meanwhile, my mother was not getting better, though she wasn't what we considered "deathly ill." I remember the first Sunday in March 1988: my mother was preparing to attend morning worship, and I'd noticed an unusual glow about her. I asked how she felt and why she seemed to be so full of joy and glowing. She just smiled as she sang with the choir on the television. As I left, I said, "I'll see you later," to which she replied, "I won't be here." I thought, *Oh yeah, it's communion*

Sunday, and you'll be home a little later. What I didn't know at the time was that she'd known otherwise; mother was actually preparing me for the worst. When I returned home from my church service, I visited a cousin who informed me that my mother had experienced a massive heart attack in church and was in the hospital.

I raced to the hospital to find my mother on life support. Her face was so contorted that I could barely recognize her. One eye was closed, and the other was open but milky-looking. Her tongue was swollen and hanging out of the side of her mouth. She was brain-dead; her body was technically alive, but steadily growing stiff and cold. *How could this happen?* I'd lost my baby, my lover, and now I was losing my mother. *God, what's next?* People prayed with me, but I didn't know what to ask God for. After all, my life was in shambles. I'd been taught that if you had not been a "good Christian," you had no right to ask God for anything. In fact I'd been told that when things like this happen, it was probably punishment from God. *Could that be true?*

Tuesday, March 8, 1988, at 2:30 AM, my mother went from labor to reward. I experienced the third of my doom's days: my mother was gone. As we prepared for the home-going service, Henry called to extend his condolences. I was almost surprised at the fact that I felt nothing for him when we talked. He told me that he wanted to do something for the family, so he was asked to sing a solo at the service. He sang and left, as I sat staring at a coffin covered in beautiful flowers, knowing my mother was gone. *What would I do? How would I make it? Who would pray me through this tough time?*

LOOKING FOR LOVE — AGAIN

In the summer of 1988, I was still trying to cope with the loss of my child, Henry and my mother. On a trip to take my vehicle to be serviced, I ran into my mechanic who'd known my mother very well. I informed him that she'd passed, and as he expressed his sympathy, we begin to talk about various subjects. Eventually, he informed me that he was attracted to me. I thought, *Why not? What do I have to lose?* This young man was thirteen years older than I was, and by then I knew enough about myself to know that I tended to be attracted to older men as a result of the relationship between my cousin and me. Regardless, I figured that this new James could possibly be the one for me and may be the man I need. I thought, *At least he's not married*, but at that point, I didn't know. We made a date for that night, and, as usual, I was intimate with him right away. I knew very little about him or his history, but I had a craving for male affection that I needed to soothe. I didn't give a second thought to whether or not he may have had a disease, a wife, or a criminal history. The opportunity presented itself, and I seized it. I was hurting, lonely, and depressed. I thought, *Why not seek after another relationship? Nothing else seems to work.*

We continued seeing each other, and immediately I wanted a commitment. I wanted him to move in, so I gave him a key to my apartment. I made him feel as if he were the "man of the house"; I enjoyed allowing him to tell me what to do. It made me feel protected and loved. I allowed him to demand things of me and from me, and he became increasingly aggressive, though not to the point of physical violence. I took care of him as if he were my husband. I washed his clothes, I cooked, and I made sure the house was clean. I found myself living a life of fantasy — but it was one he was looking to get out of.

I found myself playing the role of concubine again — this James, too, was married and a minister. The difference this time, I'd told myself, was that he had been separated from his wife for thirteen years and was planning to divorce her. *Besides*, I thought, *he spent most nights with me.* I was perpetuating my usual pattern. I was still finding myself becoming involved with men who were married, older, and who held positions in the church. It had begun at age twelve with my cousin James, and at age twenty-two, I was with a different James, but still under the same curse from my cousin James. *Did I have an obsession with these married men who had titles?* I didn't know, but in this new man I felt that I had someone who could love me as I desired to be loved. I had confused being sexually involved with being in love. I felt that if a man slept with me, it meant that he must love me. I know now that all it meant was that he had a desire, and I'd been there to fulfill it. My relationship with this new James, however, was different than the ones I'd had previously. As long as I did what he asked, we were okay. I'd begun to think that as long as I was submissive, he would desire me. In fact, the opposite was true. It didn't make him desire me; it just allowed him to take away more of my voice. I mistakenly thought that if I compromised what I believed, if I allowed him to have his way, and if I surrendered my body at his requests, he would stay.

After dating for two months, I began to feel very ill. *Could it be that I'm pregnant again?* Yes—I'd survived a miscarriage in 1987, and now in 1988, I was pregnant again. How could I tell James—especially when I knew he was struggling financially? When I mustered up enough courage to tell him, our discussion did not go well. He made the usual comments and asked the usual questions. He wanted to know how I could be sure that this was his baby. He also accused me of "trapping" him because, as he claimed, I knew he didn't want any more children. Feeling rejected once again, I went into my shell and hoped for the best. Eventually he came around and decided to live up to his responsibilities. I was relieved; I'd crossed the first hurdle.

Now I had to tell my church family, and I wasn't looking forward to it. You see, I belonged to a church that believed if you became pregnant outside of marriage, you had to be silenced —that is, removed from all of your current positions in the church until you publically apologized. I knew that eventually I'd have to subject myself to that, but I thought little of it at that moment, because I was getting the family I thought I wanted. Eventually, I learned I was having twins. I was excited and looking forward to mother-hood, even though I was ill-prepared; I knew nothing about being a mother, I had no babysitter lined up, and I knew nothing about the great expense involved with raising two babies at once. All I knew was that James and I were going to be parents, and I couldn't wait.

One night in January of 1989, I began having severe abdominal pains. I tossed and turned, but the pain steadily increased. I got up the next morning to try to use the bathroom and while I was sitting, I felt a release of fluids and the sensation of something falling out of me. It was one of my babies. Mostly bones, he had not yet formed a face, ears, fingers, or toes. He was just small enough to fit into my hand. I thought, *God what are you doing?* I was rushed to the emergency room and hospitalized. On January 8, 1989, my son was pronounced dead, and I was told that my daughter would likely not live. I was sent home that Monday and placed on bed rest. I thought, *God why is this happening to me?* James had been informed about my crisis, but apparently didn't think much about coming to see me. I stayed in the bed with a fever, not knowing whether my daughter would live.

Later, as a few friends from church were arriving to visit me, the paramedics were entering my home. I was in labor again; this time my daughter was dying. I was rushed to the emergency room again, only to learn that the baby was coming, and there was nothing the doctors could do about it. She was too premature to live. *Oh my God, I'm loosing two children in one week.* That Wednesday night, January 11, 1989, my daughter was pronounced dead. The doctors were kind enough to allow me to hold her—little Angelica Nicole. I realized how small she was, and I knew that she was mine. The nurse took her from me, and I was prepared for emergency surgery. I thought, *Where is James—home with his wife?* I knew that even though they were separated, she'd continued living in their marital house, and he would sometimes spend the night "for the kids' sake." Hadn't I heard that before?

I CAN'T TAKE ANY MORE PAIN

"Brethren, if a man be overtaken in a fault, ye which are spiritual, restore such an one in the spirit of meekness; considering thyself, lest thou also be tempted."
Galatians 6:1 (KJV)

During this dark time, I needed someone to minister healing to me. I needed to feel the love of God that so many people had talked about. In the span of eighteen months, I'd miscarried, I'd ended my relationship with Henry, and I'd lost my mother and now two more children. On top of that, my relationship with James was also dying. I thought, *God, I can't take any more pain.* The scripture says that when we are overtaken by faults, those who are spiritual are to restore us. God's message to those who have strayed away is one of love and reconciliation. While I was in the hospital—after I'd lost Angelica—many of the members of my church visited me—not to console me, but to remind me that I had sinned. They actually told me that God had killed my children because I was a fornicator. I had been made to believe that this was the kind of God I'd been serving. *But what about the other young ladies in the church who'd had babies out of wedlock? Their children had lived. Why was I different? Was there anyone who could remind me that God still loved me and could still use me in His Kingdom?* No, the church was more interested in magnifying my sin than they were in magnifying the love of God.

It didn't stop there. A special meeting was called, during which I was told that I must stand before the church, confess my sin, and ask the church to forgive me. If I refused, I would be silenced. In my pain, I reminded my accusers that my children had died, and that I needed prayer. They told me that after I asked for forgiveness, they would have someone to pray for me. They did not realize how close to breaking I was; all they wanted was for me to adhere to their policy. After an hour and a half of discussing my sin, telling me I was wrong, and demanding an apology, I refused to cooperate and would talk no further. The bishop stated that I could still attend church, but I was officially silenced.

I couldn't take it anymore; I just wanted to die. *How could life be so cruel? How could the people who said they loved God expose my pain, rather than covering me? God, how could you allow me to hurt so much?* I was tired. I went home that night and contemplated suicide. I remember praying and asking God to allow me to die in my sleep. When I awoke the next morning, I was furious that I was still alive. I took my keys and decided to drive off of a local bridge. As I was approaching the front door, I heard a bird chirping at my window, but I saw nothing. As I continued to look out of the window I heard the voice of God, say, **"If can take care of the sparrow, surely I can take care of you."** I stopped right there, knowing then that somehow God had a better plan for my life.

I continued to wait for James to get a divorce. The longer I waited, the more I found myself feeling like I was in a hole that I could not get out of. He told me that he couldn't get the divorce because of his finances. I even volunteered to pay for it, but that was to no avail. Can you believe that I wanted to be with a man who had a wife, who denied his children, who would not grieve the death of his twins, and who didn't care about me emotionally? I began to pray twisted prayers: *God give me this man even though I know he's not the one for me.* Thank God for unanswered prayers! As James became increasingly comfortable with me, he began dating other women and expected me to be okay with it. I retaliated by having relationships with other men. I knew that this was not the life for me, but after dating him for four years, I still believed he would get divorced and marry me.

THE SPIRIT IS BROKEN

I was becoming weary. I desired better, but didn't know where to start. I began to take my relationship with God a little more seriously. Going to church finally stopped being a Sunday ritual; I actually went looking for something—I wanted so much from God. I desired certain gifts of the Spirit, and I desired to be used by Him. I realized that my life was a mess, but I knew God could change all of that. In September 1992, I told James that we needed to be apart to see if we were meant to be. I asked that we not talk again until New Year's Eve to see if we still wanted the relationship. He figured that I was trying to break off the relationship because of another man, and I was—His name was Jesus. I explained that I wanted to live a life that was pleasing to God, and I thought that as a minister, he would feel the same way. He told me that my place was to please my man and that God would understand. I think his interpretation of the Word was a little different from mine.

The more I stayed away from James, the closer I drew to God. I loved my new relationship with Him. I read my Word, I prayed, and went to work in a new ministry. I also stopped using my body for ungodly pleasure. I knew I didn't want the relationship with James, but I wasn't strong enough to break it off. As New Year's Eve drew closer, I anxiously awaited his response to my ultimatum. He told me, "You are not going anywhere; no one will love you like I do." From that, I knew he had a warped sense of the meaning of love, and that I definitely didn't know what true love was. While I loved James and wanted things to work out between us, my love for God was stronger. I attended watch-night service that New Year's Eve, during which various church members stood and shared their stories of how they made it through the year. I sat silently listening, hoping that there would be a message on my answering machine when I returned. My pastor got up to preach as the clock approached midnight. His word of encouragement was entitled, "Free in '93."

It was exactly the Word I needed. It was not deep, long, or profound, but it was just what I needed to jump start me out of the mess I was in. I left church in a hurry, because I'd received a Word that had freed me to walk in my divine destiny. I called James and told him, "I love you, and want things to work out, but God has better for me. IT'S OVER!" After four years of waiting, I knew God had something else in store for me. I walked away from James and never looked back. Although there were times I longed for him, I was determined to stay free. He even went so far as to call to see if I needed him to rotate my tires or check my car's oil, because he was my mechanic. My answer was always no. I had to stay free. I knew I needed God to purge and heal me. I didn't know where to begin, but I was determined not to go back to the abuse I'd left. Sure I thought about trying to make things between us work again, but simply remembering the pain I'd suffered in the relationship was enough to clear my vision. After months of pursuing me in futility, James finally gave up, and I moved further into my new relationship with God. The "spirit of the concubine" had broken.

CHAPTER SEVEN

This Can't Happen To Me

"If you think you are standing strong, be careful not to fall."
I Corinthians 10:12 (NLT)

"Never say never." How many times have we heard this saying? How many times have you said you wouldn't do something, but later found yourself committing that very act? One thing I failed to realize during this young time in my life is that the enemy is cunning and conniving, and when it comes to war, he doesn't fight fairly. While the sexual abuse didn't cause me to commit suicide and the ungodly relationships were finally over, I didn't know that I was not yet delivered. I had walked away from it all, but I never allowed God to heal the brokenness inside. I had been taught to forget the past and move on. Shout over it and speak in tongues to exhaustion—just don't deal with the truth. We'd been taught leave the past in the past. What I did not know, however, was that if I did not confront my past, I'd never conquer it. I didn't want to become consumed by the pain of my past, but no one told me that if I did not deal with certain areas, they would come back to haunt me. The same goes for the man who refuses to deal with his anger as a child and the woman who does not deal with the rejection she felt as a teenager. If these issues are not addressed, the individuals will always battle anger and insecurity.

Once I walked away from James, I went after God with all my heart. I knew I had been called to do something, but I wasn't sure where to begin or what to do with how I felt. I was experiencing God in a different way and didn't understand what was going on. The things that once held me back were no longer a part of my life, and I was on my way. As I was listening to a televangelist one night, I heard God say to me, *"Go forth, and preach My Word." How could I do that with all of the mess that had gone on in my life?* God couldn't possibly want to use me.

What I didn't know was that God wanted to take the mess I'd been through and turn it into a ministry, because it had definitely been a miracle that I'd survived it all. When I heard this instruction from God, I immediately set up an appointment to speak with my new pastor. I thought it would be easy—that he would push me to the pulpit. It didn't happen that way, nor did it happen quickly. I thought that because I'd been called to preach and I was anointed, my pastor should have given me a date to preach my initial sermon. But he saw something that I could not see. He knew that I lacked a vital characteristic: integrity. Because I had been so hurt and was so emotionally damaged, I often dealt with others harshly. I had not yet learned to tame my tongue; I said what I wanted to say. I had no respect for leadership—especially male leadership—because of the way the church treated me regarding my lost pregnancy. I was very rebellious and disobedient. Nevertheless, I felt that since I was anointed, I should preach. What I understand now is that while my anointing could get me into ministry, it would be my integrity that would keep me there. I've met a lot of preachers with no integrity, and I didn't want to be one in the number.

My pastor was very wise. He knew that if he had released me to preach, I would have damaged more people than I helped. Because of my spiritual immaturity, I that felt my pastor was trying to hold me back. Now I know that he was only helping me to be the best minister I could be. As time went on, I began to see some of the things my pastor saw. God had also placed good friends around me to help me see the errors of my ways and to show me that I often offended people. I knew that the pain I'd suffered in the past was the cause of my actions and feelings. I could not be happy for others in their success because of jealousy; I couldn't compliment another woman because of insecurity. I had more issues than I cared to deal with. I often struggled with genuinely caring and loving others, because I had been so corrupted by what I defined as love. I realized that I had to work through all of these issues before I could be released to minister to God's people.

THE TIME HAS COME

After years of seeking God and allowing Him to purge me, my pastor began to see enough growth in me to understand the call on my life. I learned that I'd been made to wait because people would have been unable to hear what I was saying over the volume of my ungodly actions. My pastor instructed me to begin working with potential new converts, leading them to Christ. This was new for me, because when I'd dealt with new converts in my former church, we magnified the sin. We put fear in new believers when it came to salvation. We preached fire, hell, and brimstone to those seeking to accept God. So I had to relearn the Word of God so that I could teach the love of God to others, while not magnifying their sin. I learned to be careful of what I said, because I was sometimes judgmental against people who were not of the "Pentecostal faith." I also started becoming more involved in Sunday school and Bible study. Any good preacher knows that he or she needs to be taught before he or she can teach others. So I was making some progress, learning to keep my opinions to myself, and understanding that I was not the pastor; my job was to pray and intercede for him. On September 28, 1995, I preached my initial sermon, ***"Kiss Michal Goodbye."***

My gift began to make room for me, and God released me to preach and teach His Word in other churches and in many places, even other states. I was still feeling that I'd been delivered—God was moving in my life; I was celibate, those harmful men were finally out of my life, and things were good. I could actually testify about being saved and spirit-filled and know that my lifestyle matched my testimony. The feelings of lust were under control. In the past, the enemy had made me believe that I could not live without being sexually active, but I was learning that I could because of something I'd never experienced before—a relationship with God.

NOT ME!

As I continued preaching God's Word, I noticed that I only preached about certain sins. As an observant church-going child, I'd learned that part of the preacher's job was to let the congregation know that sin was prevalent in the house of God. Sometimes my sermons were focused on condemning people, rather than building them up. Like many preachers, I was stuck on one particular sin— mine was homosexuality. Regardless of my topic, the occasion, or the church, I would make sure to slip in a comment about this sin. I guess I preached so much about it because I felt that it was a sin that I'd never fall prey to. I even avoided individuals who I thought were struggling in this area. I would make smart comments about their struggles, not realizing that I could have easily been in the same dilemma. I believe this is the point that the Apostle Paul was making when he spoke to the church of Corinth, *"If you think you are standing strong, be careful not to fall."* It is possible to think that you are so strong in your faith that you can't be tempted by sin. But Paul says if you think you are standing strong—meaning standing in your own strength—be careful. I failed to apply this Word to my life, and while condemning others, I was opening the door for the enemy to attack me.

It is possible to hurt so badly from an incident that your mind actually forgets it. I call it "selective amnesia." Because the memories of being molested by my babysitter, Regina, were so painful and ugly, my mind had blocked them—as if the abuse by her had never happened. However, subliminally, I was still reaping the effects of what she had done to me, and I was still susceptible to the pattern that set those events. One thing I know about the enemy, he doesn't play fairly. When you think your life is going well—when things are finally in place and you think you are on the road to success—he will bring something up to detour your walk. While preaching so adamantly against homosexuality, I found myself struggling with that very issue. *No, not me! Whom could I tell that I was having lesbian thoughts? Whom could I tell that I no longer desired to be with a man but with a woman? Where were these feelings coming from? How could I be a preacher and have these desires? God, this can't be happening to me!*

I felt like an animal trapped in a cage. I was embarrassed, afraid, disappointed, and confused, and felt I had no one who could counsel me. After all, people had begun looking to me for guidance—to set the Godly example and to be their role model—yet I was struggling. I'd allowed myself to be placed on a pedestal to the extent that others felt that I was unaffected by sin. That's a bad place to allow people to put you; only God is superior to sin and its effects. I struggled, I cried, and I contemplated giving in—all while continuing to preach. I was experiencing first hand what the people I'd been preaching against must have felt. I was miserable; I feared that I was becoming one of "them," and I had no one to turn to.

I became very paranoid around other women, making sure not to offend or to come across as though I was "hitting" on them. The desire to be with a woman eventually became so strong that I found myself in a fetal position, crying before God to take the desire away. I knew it was not God's desire for me to be a lesbian, but the feelings were becoming overwhelming. I didn't know what to do, and I didn't know whom I could trust with this information. However, I did know that I needed help—desperately.

THE SECRET IS OUT

One thing I've found: the more you try to hide from something, the more paranoid you become about everything. Because I'd become so concerned with hiding my secret desires, I missed out on the fact that I had good friends who would not judge me, but who would understand and counsel me regarding my struggle. I believe that if I had applied the Word to my situation, I could have saved myself a lot of heartache and stress. The book of James declares, **"Confess your faults one to another, and pray one for another, that ye may be healed. The effectual fervent prayer of a righteous man availeth much,"** (James 5:16 [KJV]). I only looked at my struggle as "sinful"; I didn't understand that I needed more healing from the sexual abuse I'd suffered as a child. Thus, I continued to hide. There were many nights I cried out to God for deliverance. I had asked Him to send me someone who could minister to me, but when He did, I rejected the help. Because God didn't respond in the manner I thought He would, I didn't recognize my deliverance. As I was crying out to God in the night, He would send one of my friends to my house to minister to me, but I wouldn't open the door. I was too ashamed to deal with what I was going through. I'd allowed the enemy to bring condemnation to me, along with a spirit of pride.

I knew I couldn't continue living like this, so I decided that if my friends were true friends, they would be there for me. I braced myself and confessed my sins to them, and they politely said, "We know." They never judged me, and they never stopped loving me. They got me through my tough times with the compassion and love of God. In ministering to me, my friends called forth my inner strength and would not allow me to have a "pity party." They challenged me in love. They spoke the truth and even encouraged me to seek counseling if I felt that I needed it. Because I availed myself to receive healing and deliverance, I did. God used these women of God to speak such powerful words in me that when the enemy came with that temptation, the word of God spoke against it. They were friends indeed.

TAKE HEED

As I continued ministering at singles' and women's conferences, I knew that when I shared my testimony, the enemy would despise being exposed and would be determined to keep me quiet. While I was walking in my deliverance from lesbian thoughts and being healed from the sexual abuse, it did not stop the enemy. The Bible tells us that when Jesus was in the wilderness, the enemy left Him for a season and later returned to tempt Jesus again. Often, we think that when the enemy is not attacking, the fight is over. I've learned that he's only gone back to the board room to pull up another plan of attack and will return at another time. When I shared my experiences with sexual abuse, there were times when I could feel the spirit of lesbianism in the room. If I prayed for a woman who was struggling, I had to ensure I was covered spiritually to prevent the enemy from attacking me again.

As I traveled and preached, the enemy was planning another attack. I had to "take heed," remembering that if I stood on my own strength, I would definitely fall. I was invited to preach at a church one Sunday morning, and the pastor informed me that a particular woman had been overcome by an ungodly spirit. The Sunday prior to my being there, she had been in the aisle barking like a dog. The woman was in the service on this particular morning, as well, but this time she was not barking. This day, her assignment was to approach me, because she had previously been in a lesbian relationship. During the altar call, she began to act out. I had to keep my focus and stick to my assignment. Sometimes ignoring a spirit is a direct rebuke, because if the enemy can redirect your focus from the Almighty God onto him, then his job is done. So as she continued to be disruptive, the ministers took this woman out of the service, so that I could continue ministering to God's people. However, at the conclusion of the service, while I was preparing to leave, the enemy returned. The woman walked up to me and asked me to touch one of her private body parts. That homosexual spirit was trying to entice me again. Of course, I rebuked the spirit and never looked back. So take heed: don't think that the enemy won't come back to entice you, *even if you think your struggle is far behind you.*

CHAPTER EIGHT

Silence Strengthens the Hand of the Abuser

"Brethren, I count not myself to have apprehended: but this one thing I do, forgetting those things which are behind, and reaching forth unto those things which are before,"
Philippians 3:13 (KJV)

I believe that at one time or another, we all have heard these state-ments: *Don't bring up the past; leave things alone; don't deal with your past, just keep moving forward.* Well, I believe these words of advice may be valid in some instances, but often they are taken out of context. I remember when I was grieving the death of my twins, I had a hard time being around infants or attending baby showers. I had even been told by some church members to forget about my babies, because it was demonic to grieve. These people had led me to believe that God had killed my children because I'd fornicated; therefore, I had no right to grieve their deaths. *How cruel!* Do you realize how many children we'd have to bury if that was God's punishment for fornication? I believed this lie, nonetheless, and I did not properly grieve the death of my twins; I simply tried to move on. I tried to forget those things that were behind me—but in my heart, I couldn't.

I believe it is important to take scripture in its full context. In Philippians 3:13, Paul was not suggesting that we should act as though we've never been through negative experiences. Rather, he was saying that we should not dwell on these events to the point that we cannot move on to the present. The process of forgiveness in itself is one that requires us to deal with our past. I am a firm believer now that you can't conquer what you won't confront. So I was wrong in trying to *forget* all of my pain. By acting as if it didn't exist, I had been hindered from moving forward.

I began to realize that I'd suffered severe sexual abuse from the age of five to the age of nineteen. Because of the all the bad advice I'd received over the years, I didn't know where to look to receive the help I needed. Some of my acquaintances told me to "just turn it over to the Lord, and let Him work it out." That's a cliché that is useless to a struggling believer. How do I turn over my nightmares, my anger, my pain, my vengefulness, and my inability to forgive to the Lord? No one could tell me. Many went back to the old Pentecostal ritual of trying to rebuke the pain; others told me to turn around three times and I'd be healed. Of course, none of this worked. I'd begun to wonder whether God Himself could help me. I was in so much pain that I sometimes even questioned whether I was mentally sound: I could be a very nice, giving, and caring person one moment, but then I could be "hell on wheels" the next. Nothing in particular triggered these personality swings—at least I didn't think so at the time.

THE TRUTH IS REVEALED

There had to be reasons for my actions. *Why was I so rebellious toward leadership, especially male leadership?* Whenever it seemed as though a male was trying to control me, I'd often rebel against him in a very aggressive manner. According to some, I was being disrespectful. Others didn't know what to think of the "church girl with the foul mouth." I could claim Jesus in one moment, and then curse you the next. *What was my problem?*

One day in 1998, I was watching a televangelist who shared her testimony of sexual abuse and bad behavior patterns as a result. As I listened, I noticed that she and I had a lot in common, and I thought it was mighty brave of her to share this with so many people. After all, I'd been told to keep personal business in my house when I was growing up. Why would someone want the world to know they had been abused? Why put yourself out there like that? What I didn't know was that *silence strengthens the hand of the abuser.* Many pedophiles continue their lifestyle because no one ever confronts or exposes them. There are many reasons that victims don't come forth, but this evangelist had no problems sharing her story. As she spoke, I noticed that my pain began to erupt; I remembered every incident, and I became angry. The truth had been revealed. I needed healing for all of the abuse I'd suffered. Regardless of what I was being told by those who were uncomfortable by the situation, I had to confront these demons in my life or I would never walk in my divine destiny.

<u>WHO WILL BELIEVE ME?</u>

I had not been in a relationship since 1993, and as 1998 approached, I had begun feeling pretty good about being in ministry and being obedient to the call of God on my life. My pastor would often preach about becoming whole in God, having balance, and walking in your destiny. While I said amen, I knew that I was not yet whole. I scheduled an appointment with my pastor to share my concerns about my past and to get some advice about how to handle it. He gave me Godly counsel and told me that I did not need profes-sional counseling unless I felt that I had reached a point from which I could not move on. While, as an adult, I walked confidently in my calling, there was still an inner child in me, crying out to be healed. Most people saw the strong me; however, I saw the damaged me, and I knew I had to do something. I had been given custody of my great niece in 1997, and I'd noticed that I had taken on an unhealthy way of protecting her from life. I've learned that victims of sexual abuse can have a myriad of reactions when they become parents. They can begin to trust everyone with their children, or they can do the exact opposite—like I did—and trust no one. Only a few victims are able to have healthy, balanced lives. These individuals are those who have been healed and delivered from their yokes of bondage.

I finally made a decision the spring of 2000 to share my sexual abuse with my siblings. I knew it would not be easy, but I needed the support of my family to deal with what I'd been through. Additionally, I knew I needed some type of professional counseling, but I was not sure how I would handle the emotional stress of it all. So I decided to take things one step at a time. I wrote letters to my siblings, telling them my story. I also wrote a letter to my cousin James to inform him that I was going public with the truth about the abuse. As I was writing him, I remember trying to tell him the same thing long ago. His response had been, "They won't believe you; you are just a child." Well I had become an adult with some serious problems, who needed to be healed. *Who would believe me now?*

WHO OPENED THAT CAN OF WORMS?

After I sent out the letters, I didn't know what my family's reaction would be. All I knew was that I needed to get this mess out of me, because my silence was strengthening those who had abused me. I was not sure if my cousin had done this to any of my other family members, but I knew what he had done to me. After reading my letters, my siblings were devastated. They each had different responses, but the two that affected me the most came from my two older sisters. The eldest took it pretty hard and was advised by her therapist to refrain from discussing her feelings until she had healed and the anger had subsided. Somehow, she felt totally responsible for the incidents because of her own childhood experiences. So we didn't hear anything from her for a while. My second eldest sister was very nonchalant and felt that I should have kept quiet about it all. It's so easy for others to say, "If it had been me..." but until one has walked in the hurting person's shoes, sometimes the best way to be supportive is to keep quiet. Needless to say, her response didn't go over very well with my other siblings. By the time all was said and done, my family members were at each others' throats. *What had I done in opening this can of worms?*

I remember as a youngster, I loved watching "The McCoys and the Hatfields." The show was based on feuding neighbors, and from what I could gather, this feud had been going on for years. Well their fights had nothing on my family, once my secret was out. Although I was not trying to hurt my family, it had turned out that way. My eldest sister, acting out of her emotions, wanted to ensure that justice was served. She spoke with my cousin on several occasions and needless to say, they did not have pleasant conversations. Their arguments spilled over to other family members and before any of us could regain control of the situation, the worms of discord were out of the can and crawling everywhere. *My God, I never meant for this to happen; I just wanted to be healed and move on.* Some of my family members told me that I should have remained quiet; others said I'd gotten what I deserved. There were only a few who empathized with me, who were sickened and angered by the whole ordeal. Either way, I had exposed my cousin's actions, but in the process, I'd become an outcast in my family.

A week after receiving my letter, my cousin finally called me to discuss the issue. I thought his initial conversation would be one of repentance and remorse, but it was nowhere near that. His concern was his reputation—what the "church folks" would think of him and whether I planned to tell his wife. I felt that it was his decision; after all, I was not out to defame his character. Hopefully, with the whole matter out in the open, it would make him see the error of his ways and get the help he needed, as well.

TO THINE OWN SELF BE TRUE

It's one thing to lie to others, but it's really sad when you lie to yourself and believe it. While recounting the events of what had happened between us, my cousin had somehow come to believe that we'd had an affair and that *I'd* seduced *him*. I became furious trying to explain to him that you cannot have an affair with a child. I reminded him that I was twelve and he was forty-two when these events began—that is not an affair. He told me that all he remembered was that I wanted to be with him and that I'd turned him on.

What was it about me, at the age of twelve, that could possibly have turned him on? Twelve-year-old girls in the seventies looked a lot different than they do today. He was adamant that I had initiated everything and he refused to see that he was a pedophile. He questioned my motives in waiting so long to go public about what had happened. He was convinced that I was out to get him and to ruin his family. Not one time did he see the error of his ways. He didn't understand that it was perverted to be intimate with your first cousin. He was totally aloof about the fact that he'd taken my virginity, and he was totally oblivious to what he had done to me mentally and emotionally. I was waiting for some type of apology or admission of guilt, but I received none. After a half hour of such an unproductive conversation, I could no longer tolerate listening to him.

Though I tried desperately to get him to apologize and admit that we'd not "simply" had an affair, I also had to be truthful with myself. Although this all began when I was twelve, I had to admit that by a certain age I was accountable for my own decisions and actions. At some point, I knew that what we were doing was wrong, and I should have put a stop to it. I even told James this in hopes that he, too, would admit his wrongdoings, but that didn't work either. He was totally convinced that we'd had an affair.

Meanwhile, James was still battling my eldest sister. She'd called his pastor to tell him what had happened; she insisted that some type of reprimand be given. His pastor was shocked to learn that a man of James' caliber would be guilty of such a charge. My sister then began to demand that James tell the family what he'd done to me and apologize. He did tell some family members what he'd done, but what he told them was not the truth. My family members were led to believe that these events had occurred while I was an adult, which caused them to feel that I'd gotten what I deserved.

For some reason, James could not bring himself to say that he had engaged in pedophilic activities with me. When he'd discussed the issue with his wife, he'd told her we'd had an affair. The anger and hate began to eat away at me. I felt that before I could forgive him, he had to say the magic words: "I am a pedophile." But he continued to call it an affair, and the more he did, the more I despised him. I lived with this hatred every day; I pondered it, and found ways to hate him even more. Before long, I was consumed by the hate I had for James. I even considered doing bodily harm and pleading insanity. I wanted justice and my abuser was refusing to give it to me. It became too much to handle. I needed to press toward my future, but I was stuck in my past.

FORGIVENESS IS A "MUST"

After months of dealing with the pain that had resulted from telling my story; and after watching my family nearly fall apart, I knew I had to find a way to forgive him. While I understood the Word of God as it pertained to forgiving, I felt that God would understand that I couldn't forgive, because my pain was so deep. I'd been through many bad relationships as a result of the abuse I'd experienced, and my constant seeking after married men was derived from the relationship I'd had with my cousin James. As I shared my emotional turmoil with a friend, she said, "You know, you have to forgive him before you can move on." I became livid; she couldn't be serious. *How could I be expected to forgive James after what he'd done to me?*

I started keeping myself busy so that I wouldn't think about the situation. I told myself that there was more joy in hating him than in forgiving him. While my friends continued to minister to me, telling me that I should forgive, I refused to take their advice and found ways to justify my pain and hurt. One night while I was cleaning my house (one of my ways of hiding), the Holy Spirit spoke and told me that I had to deal with this. I remember slinging my broom across the room, running to the sofa, and pleading with God to show me how to forgive James and my other abusers.

God met me at that moment, and I knew I had let go of the hatred. The Spirit continued to deal with me about forgiving James even as I ministered at a singles' conference. Afterward, the pastor came to me and gave me a word of encouragement. He told me that as long as I held on to the pain, I was tying God's hands in my situation. Yes, God would deal with James, but not until I released what I'd been holding on to. You see, I believed that if I forgave James, I would be sending him the message that what he'd done to me was okay. But I was wrong. That's not what forgiving someone is all about.

I had to first understand that forgiving is a principle of God found in Matthew 6:14 (KJV): *"For if ye forgive men their trespasses, your heavenly Father will also forgive you."* This scripture cut me deeply, because it meant that not only was I holding onto a grudge, but it meant that I was also holding up my ministry and my blessings, and I was killing my destiny. Then I read verse fifteen: *"But if ye forgive not men their trespasses, neither will your Father forgive your trespasses."* That meant that regardless of what my cousin had done, what he'd said, or how my family had responded, I still had to forgive. So, the day after I preached at the singles' conference, I wrote James a letter telling him that I forgave him. I believe that this not only freed me, but it released God to deal with my cousin according to His will and not according to my desire. Although I didn't know the whereabouts of my other abusers, I forgave them as well.

James never apologized, nor did he respond to my letter. I knew that if I wanted to move on, his response (or lack of response) had to become unimportant. I had wasted so much time over the course of my life; I didn't want to waste anymore time by walking in an inability to forgive. I came to the realization that I would be okay regardless of whether he admitted that he had abused me or not. I had to tell myself that if he never apologized and if my family never supported me, I would still be okay. I made myself content with the fact that he'd been exposed; he was unable to hurt me anymore.

CHAPTER NINE

Who Am I?

*"Therefore if any man be in Christ, he is a new creature: old
things are passed away; behold, all things are become new."*
II Corinthians 5:17 (KJV)

*W*ho *is this new creature, and how can I get all of these old
things to pass away?* I used to feel so discombobulated and
worthless that I pondered at times if God would ever be able to
restore me. While I preached the gospel that set others free, I was
bound. I had trained myself to smile when I was hurting, to shout
when I didn't really feel like it, and to say "Praise the Lord!" when
I wanted to scream, "Somebody help me!" I felt like I was trapped
in a body with an individual that I didn't know. *How do I begin to
put things behind me and allow myself to become a new creature?* I
knew my heart was new, that I'd developed relationship with Christ,
but I still had the residue of the old stuff in me.

Who was I? How could I preach so powerfully, encourage others,
sing, and enjoy ministry, and at the end of it all, go home, look at
my life and ask, "Can these dry bones live?" A part of me regretted
exposing the enemy, because now I had to deal with the demons. It
was far harder than I ever thought it would be. I'd shared my story
with my siblings, exposed the truth, and still I was the outcast of my

family. I no longer felt comfortable at family functions, and it felt as if my life was slowly ending. *There must be some help somewhere.*

I understood that the old things would pass away when I became new in Christ. It wasn't that I was unsaved, I just had to learn to see myself through God's eyes. I had to stop looking at myself in a shameful way; I had to stop thinking that I was only good in the bedroom; and I had to stop feeling worthless. If I failed to do so, I would be invalidating the work of the cross. Jesus died so that I could be free from the abuse and its residual effects. I now had to walk in that freedom. Taking that first step was not easy, but it was the only way to initiate this life-saving process.

I NEED HELP

I remember some years ago, a televangelist fell to sexual sin. He admitted that it had been a problem for him for years. He admitted that it began with looking at pornographic movies and magazines and had progressed to fantasies about being with numerous women at the same time. He pondered these thoughts until he actually had fallen prey to the sin. What he hadn't realized from the start was that where his mind went, his body would follow. I watched him publicly ask for forgiveness, and I wondered if he understood that his problem was deeper than mere fantasies. I admired this televangelist, because he could have walked in pride and refused to repent, denying that he'd done anything wrong.

Sometimes the enemy tricks us into believing that our titles place us above repenting and seeking the help we need. That minister probably felt as I had on several occasions. Asking the questions, "Whom can I tell about my struggle?" "Who would understand that I have a great anointing on my life, while still struggling with serious internal issues?" Paul laments in Romans 7:19–20 (KJV), ***"For the good that I would I do not: but the evil which I would not, that I do. Now if I do that I would not, it is no more I that do it, but sin that dwelleth in me."*** While trying to do what's right, Paul found himself struggling with evil. Oh, how well I knew that feeling! My intentions had been good, but somehow the desire to "save face" was stronger at times. I knew I needed some help. After all, I couldn't keep using my abuse as an excuse for my bad behavior or unwise decisions.

For years I had been working with girls' groups in various churches and local agencies. Ironically, I spoke to them about having positive self-esteem, while I struggled with my own; I talked about saving oneself for marriage, while I'd often slipped and fell to fornication. I shared my story with one of my church friends, and she recommended a Christian ministry to me. It was structured for those who were struggling with sexual issues. *Finally, some help,* I thought and I sought out the help of the group. The first step was an eight-week program, during which we would share from a small booklet and then sit in group prayer. The group never pressured me to share my story, and no one judged me, but people who loved the word of God showed me how to apply it to my scars. We were often told to "leave our pain at the foot of the cross." This was something I'd never heard before, so I had no idea how to actually do it. I figured, though, that if I hung around this group long enough, I would find out. I felt safe with these people, and I knew this was what God designed to aid in the start of my healing. Still, I needed something more to get to those deeply scarred places that I was still protecting.

As I prayerfully continued with this healing ministry, I joined their next level of counseling, a forty-week program. This began a long period of counseling in which I was required to confront all of the inner pain. The sessions would pull so much out of me that sometimes I felt that I could no longer go on. I underwent extensive counseling and small-group therapy. We would come together for praise and worship, we'd study our lesson, and then we'd break into teams with our group leaders. The praise and worship periods really ministered to me; I began to use them as my time to reflect upon the reasons I was there, and why I needed to go through such a painful process. I remember a song that carried me through the most painful times:

"Open the eyes of my heart, Lord, I want to see you,
High and lifted up, shining in the light of your Glory
Pour out your power and LOVE as we sing Holy, Holy, Holy!"

I had to learn to see God as being high and lifted up above all of the abuse I'd encountered. I had to remember that He was sovereign over my situation and in charge of everything that I was going through. I had to see Him as the Almighty God.

When I first joined the group, I would sit quietly and allow the other women to share their painful stories. Although we had all been in similar situations, a part of me held on to being the "preacher" who couldn't let them know that I had issues. But the more comfortable I became, I realized that it was okay to share a little at a time. I had to reevaluate my purpose for coming: *If I was not going to allow myself to be ministered to, why had I come?* After all, these women did not know me and only saw me once a week. We never used full names, just our first names. I quickly came to the realization that if I was there to receive healing, it was imperative for me to open up; otherwise I would be wasting everyone's time.

The night I decided to share my story, I told them about the death of my twins. It seemed that our lesson that night dealt with grief, and I had a lot inside. I shared how disrespectful I'd been to male leadership and the hatred I felt toward pastors as a result of what had happened to me. The women embraced me; they talked with me about my issues, and spoke the Word of God over my pain. They also showed me where I'd gone wrong and encouraged me to seek God for healing. I thought, *This is what I've needed!*

While I was attending counseling, I was still at odds with my family. A few of my friends disagreed with my decision to seek Christian counseling, but I had to do what I felt was right for me. As we approached the end of our therapeutic sessions, I realized that the therapy had made a difference in my life, but I also knew that there were still some things I needed to deal with. Group counseling was what I called "digging up the grave." "Opening the coffin" was where I found the real issues I needed to deal with.

THE SKELETON IS OUT OF THE CLOSET

After I graduated from the program, I returned as a volunteer to assist others in their healing. I continued making progress, but I still had some serious issues to overcome—like my issues with food. The enemy had made me believe that if I remained overweight (more than 300 pounds), I wouldn't be abused again, because men were not attracted to heavy women. I believed that lie for a while, but one day it occurred to me that I'd always been heavy, and the men I dated never had a problem with my weight. What I'd believed about my size was a lie that I'd allowed the devil to tell me; he wanted to keep me in bondage so that I would not receive my healing. Sometimes the emotional pain was so intense that I just couldn't deal with it. But I knew that in order to walk in my full destiny and fulfill the call on my life, I had to go through with seeking the additional help I needed.

I had made substantial progress with counseling. I could see a change in my attitude towards pastors and men; I was no longer battling insecurity; and I was being validated in the Word of God, but I still needed some help. Sometimes I felt as if I had so many issues that I would never be healed. I even tried to talk myself out of continuing the process. I had to encourage myself, remembering that God intended for me to be whole, not broken. He wanted me to be able to walk in His perfect will, not His permissive will. Though I realized this, I still found myself seeking approval from certain people in my life. I also looked to be completed by others, especially men. Eventually, it became apparent to me that after all the counseling, I was still not completely delivered.

In 2002, I became determined to deal with the residue of my sexual abuse. My weight had become a major concern—I was "morbidly obese." When I had a problem, I ate; when I was in trouble, I ate; whenever I had a confrontation, was feeling sad, or didn't know what to do, I ate. At my heaviest, I tipped the scales at an unhealthy three hundred and forty-seven pounds. In April of that same year, I'd received a call that my twenty-four-year-old nephew had passed away. He was more than four hundred pounds. I knew that if I didn't do something, I could be next. I had gone through counseling; I knew how to deal with my issues, but I couldn't seem to conquer my hunger. I returned from my nephew's funeral, knowing that I had to do something about my weight; I could no longer use my standard excuses. After all, I was a spirit-filled, on-fire preacher, able to cast out unclean spirits. *How could I not have power over a pork chop?*

I sought help from a new physician, who told me that I had a plethora of health problems because of my weight. My doctor, who is also a Christian, suggested the gastric-bypass surgery. I thought that I couldn't possibly go that route. I'd been told that because of my medical history, I could only lose a certain amount of weight before my metabolism would stop working properly. I was told that there was medication for this problem, but that I couldn't take it due to my hypertension. I felt like I'd been backed into a corner and thought, *What am I going to do?* I prayed and sought God about the best decision for me. And after doing so, God released me to have the surgery on December 11, 2002.

Once I started losing weight things began to change. Because I had been heavy all my life, I did not know how to deal with this "new" me. Others who'd had the surgery had been encouraged by their physicians to undergo psychiatric evaluations to ensure that they could handle such a major change. My insurance carrier did not require this, so I didn't bother with it. As a result, I experienced emotional ups and downs that I didn't always know how to handle: I wasn't sure how to accept the compliments—I loved the way I looked, but I had to watch how I carried myself around men even more closely. There were times when I began to feel those old desires to be "the other woman" resurface, and I began to desire male affection again. I felt more flirtatious than ever and had to closely watch everything I did.

I started loving everything about myself: the new hair, the new body, and the new attitude. I no longer shopped at the plus-size stores; now I could shop at regular stores and choose my size without having to try the item on to ensure it would fit. Life was wonderful! I felt like I was on top of the world. Nothing could touch me, and my confidence had definitely gotten a boost. After all these years of wearing sizes in the twenties, I was finally down to a size ten and looking great. But to my amazement, no one was showing any interest in me. It started to look as though I'd been more attractive when I was heavier. While I received many compliments about my weight loss and how good I looked, I was still saddened somewhat. I battled thoughts of losing weight and still being alone. Had I dealt with who I really was, or was I still trying to find my identity? Why had I lost this weight? Was it for health reasons or to gain attention from men? I not only battled my feelings about the lack of male attention—taking it as a sign of having become unattractive—but again I battled that demon of being attracted to other women.

While I didn't say it out of my mouth, inside I was beginning to crave attention—any kind of attention. Well that was enough to give the enemy the room he needed to launch another attack. The attack was a subtle attempt to get me to use my body for sexual favors again. I began to cry out to God, reminding myself that He had brought me too far to allow me to go back. I knew that I didn't need to be in a relationship with anyone; what I needed was to continue going forward in my healing process. There was a call on my life to minister healing to women. Involving myself in any type of relationship would hinder me from realizing my divine destiny. After all, I was not yet healed enough or emotionally stable enough to deal with the ups and downs of a relationship.

In January 2004, I contacted a local Christian therapist, hoping that I could get some relief from what I was experiencing. At my first appointment, I sat in the office wondering, *When am I going to learn? What is going on with me? Why can't I get myself together?* What I didn't know was that when you begin to deal with the pain of the past, you must deal with all of it. Otherwise, what you refuse to deal with will soon come up one way or another. So I began the next phase of my journey, which lasted from January 2004 until March 2005.

I QUIT!

There were some days when I felt as though I would not make it; some days, I didn't even want to make it. My first session began with small talk, as I gave the doctor information about what I'd been experiencing. She diagnosed me with "Post Traumatic Stress," meaning that whenever something negative happened to me, the pain of my past would resurface, causing my body to react with stress attacks. It would also cause me to revert back to my old ways. I became very comfortable with my therapist, and I had no hesitations about sharing my life's story with her. I did not have to put on the well composed face, nor did I have to wear any titles. Most times, I just sat in the chair with my legs crossed, crying, and remembering the pain I'd encountered over my lifetime.

Many times the little girl in me would come out, as the tears I'd withheld for so many years were finally shed. When, I'd gotten it all out and began to feel that I could actually recover, my therapist said, "We need to take this to another level." I panicked. My mind reverted to the time when my cousin James had said the same thing, marking the beginning of a life of promiscuity for me. But she calmed me, explaining that I would be undergoing theophostic therapy, which requires the patient to relive the incident, but to see Jesus standing there during the experience.

I must admit that there were times when these sessions seemed unbearable. I would walk away in a daze, and sometimes I couldn't sleep at night. In one session, as I dealt with the death of my twins, the enemy placed a spirit of condemnation upon me. During my pregnancy, I'd taken a couple of laxatives in an effort to abort the babies, and thus I'd begun to feel guilty of causing their death. I deemed it more appropriate to kill the babies then to go through the ridicule of my church. While my therapist tried to convince me that it would take more than two laxatives to kill the twins, the enemy had convinced me otherwise. *What kind of mother would try to abort her children?* I fought with this question for weeks before I was able to place it at the foot of the cross. I felt that I deserved some type of punishment for what I'd attempted to do. What I failed to understand at that time was that God does not condemn us or make us feel bad because we've done something wrong. God wants us healed and restored. This is why He sent His grace and mercy. Thankfully, I got through that session, which let me know that I could confront the remaining ordeals in my life.

After one session of dealing with the rape, however, I made a decision to quit. Reliving those memories was just too hard; I'd started to tell myself that my life wasn't *that* bad. Right then, God revealed to me that women of various races, ages, and backgrounds were depending on my testimony to get through their own ordeals. I realized that God had allowed me to go through these traumatic events, because in the end I would give Him all of the glory. He also knew that I was strong enough to endure. There were some who watched me go through all of this, who wondered how I'd made it—*how could I forgive my abusers and still love them?* They knew that God had allowed me to go through this. So with this in mind, I returned to therapy, so that other women could receive their healing and have their faith in God restored.

Still, the journey was difficult. I often wondered, *God, when will this be over?* I even resorted to taking doses of vicodin to numb my brain. I would lie in bed not knowing what was going on around me or where I was. Depression began to set in and I thought (as did others), *If therapy caused these side affects, why go through it?* What I came to realize was that the therapy didn't cause this. Rather, I was the cause, as I'd refused to place my pain at the foot of the cross. Once I realized this, therapy became easier and easier over time. It started to become less traumatic to talk about the abuse and to remember how it had made me feel. I dealt with the issues of feeling unworthy, feeling like less of a woman, and feeling that I existed only to please men sexually. I begin to understand that I was made in the image of God and He had a purpose for my life. On a daily basis I had to denounce the lies of the enemy and come into agreement with what God has spoken over my life. During these months of therapy, God continued to use me to preach the gospel. In March 2005, God released me from therapy. A new day had dawned.

After everything I'd been through—the pain, the frustration, the mistakes, and the heartaches—I was finally walking in my healing. I knew that it didn't mean that I would never struggle again, or that the enemy would never try to make me return to the past. Rather, I knew that my healing meant that what had once conquered me, I had now overcome by the power of Jesus Christ.

I have forgiven my abusers. I have redeveloped a family-level relationship with my cousin James, and I recently felt strong enough to attend a family reunion. God has taken what I thought to be a mess, and turned it into a miracle. In July 2005, God allowed me to birth G. L. Hines Ministries, a healing ministry that allows me to travel, sharing the love of Jesus Christ. I let women across the country know that they can be healed from the demonic residue of sexual abuse. Through my testimony, God uses me to show women that "there is hope after abuse." God has also allowed me to minister along-side my therapist to other women who have been sexually abused. We've shared information to radio talk-show listeners in hopes of preventing some child from encountering the pain I experienced.

From the age of five until I was nineteen, I was sexually abused. From the age of twenty-one until age thirty, I was in and out of promiscuous relationships. From the age of thirty until I was thirty–seven, I spent countless hours seeking deliverance from it all. Now, at the age of forty-three, I finally understand that I am indeed a new creature in Christ. Yes, the old things have finally passed away. I know who I am and whose I am: I am the righteousness of God through Christ Jesus; I am the head and not the tail; I am above only and not beneath; I am a precious daughter of Zion, a vessel of honor. The things the devil tried to use to destroy me, God has taken and turned into a miracle—a powerful ministry! Most of all, God has shown me that there has been a plan for my life from the beginning. *I am NOT a mistake; I am meant to be!*

CHAPTER TEN

Undoing the Damage

"And Jesus went about all the cities and villages, teaching in their synagogues, and preaching the gospel of the kingdom, and healing every sickness and every disease among the people."
Matthew 9:35 (KJV)

You may think that you are damaged beyond restoration. I know that feeling. For a long time, I thought that I would be miserable forever. When I read Matthew 9:35, I realized that Jesus came to heal everything. We sometimes limit the concept of healing to physical illnesses, such as cancer, hypertension, and diabetes. But we must realize that Jesus came to provide for our *holistic* health; He wants our minds, emotions, and bodies to be whole. Therefore, if we are broken, damaged, torn, untrusting, or emotionally disturbed, Jesus came to heal those areas, as well. For every person who's been a victim of sexual abuse, I pray that my testimony has opened the door to healing, so that you can walk into your destiny. While the residues of abuse are real, the power of God is even more real to those who believe.

How do you undo the damage of sexual abuse? How do you begin to trust again? How do you live a normal life without the expectation that everyone will abuse you? Where does life begin for those who have been deeply wounded? If you have asked these or similar questions, you are not alone. The prophet Jeremiah felt the same way when he asked, *"Is there no balm in Gilead; is there no physician there? why then is not the health of the daughter of my people recovered?"* (Jeremiah 8:22 [KJV]). If you're like me, you've probably also asked these questions concerning your own desire for healing: *God, since you are omnipresent, couldn't you have stopped the abuse? You are omniscient—you knew this was coming—why didn't you intervene sooner? God, why did you permit what you could have prevented? Why do I hurt so much? Why do I have to go through this? Why is there so much pain left over? Are you ever going to heal me?*

<u>DESIRE HEALING</u>

One thing we must understand about healing is that although God brings it about, we have a part to play in it, as well. I've found that behind every symptom, there is a root problem. Have you ever met an older person who was mean and bitter? If you were to talk with that person long enough, you would discover that at the root of the bitterness, there is some type of unresolved pain. At some point in that person's life, he or she was hurt, but no one attended to the damage that had been caused. It's like having a deep cut that required stitches, but which was only bandaged.

I remember as a youngster, my mother didn't deal with emotional pain. She was taught by her mother that "your business is *your* business." Do not tell anyone what you are going through, just deal with it. If someone was known to be in an abusive marriage, that person would be encouraged to stay in the relationship as long as the spouse was paying the bills. If there was infidelity, the woman would be told that cheating is just something all men do. If someone was being verbally abused, the individual would be reminded of the old adage, "Sticks and stones may break your bones, but names will never harm you." We all know that this statement can't be further from the truth; there *is* power in words. Sometimes verbal abuse can be the worst abuse one can encounter.

For the percentage of women who experienced being touched inappropriately by well-thought-of family members, the advice was even worse. If the abuser was popular in the family, the victim would often be sworn to secrecy, and if she told anyway, no one believed her. For this reason, many women have kept quiet and have simply grown up knowing that something was wrong inside. They lived with the frustration of being unable to identify the root of problem. As a victim of abuse, you must recognize the need for healing, and once you do, you must pray and ask God for His guidance when choosing the method of healing that is right for you. While there were some who believed that I did not need professional therapy, only I knew what I was dealing with and the pain I was enduring. When considering your path for healing you *must* seek God, because each case is different.

ACCOUNTABILTY PARTNER

While I dealt with my sexual abuse, I found it useful to have an accountability partner. It was not easy to deal with all of the pain alone, and thus having this resource was necessary for my healing. I had developed many unhealthy behaviors, because I'd been sexually abused. I was insecure and jealous; I lacked self-esteem, and I was addicted to various sexual behaviors. I knew that if I wanted total healing, I needed someone I could trust, with whom I could share my feelings when I encountered one of these problems. Over my life-time, I had taught myself to retreat when trouble approached. This time, God sent me some wonderful friends who held me account-able for completing the healing process.

James 5:16 (KJV) says, *"Confess your faults one to another, and pray one for another that ye may be healed…"* This is one concept that is lacking in the body of Christ, because there has been so much betrayal amongst believers. Individuals who are already in severe emotional pain don't want to be hurt anymore; therefore, they hold their pain inside and do not seek out the healing they need. Truthfully, there were times when I felt unable to confess my faults because of pride or because it just hurt too much. But I remembered something my mother told me a long time ago, "Anything worth having will not come easy." Over time, I learned that this statement especially pertained to my emotional healing. My accountability partners were spiritually seasoned women of God who loved me and who were committed to seeing me complete my healing process.

ACCEPT RESPONSIBILITY IF NEEDED

In most cases of abuse, only the abuser is at fault; very rarely are there cases where the victim has done anything wrong. While many of the acts committed against me were not my fault, I had to deal with the hard truth that once I reached a certain age, I became accountable for the part I'd played. When my cousin began molesting me at age twelve, I was not yet old enough to fully understand the truth or to clearly discern between right and wrong. I really did think that he was in love with me and that there was nothing wrong with that. As I grew older and became aware that it was unnatural for cousins to be intimate with each other, I became accountable. It might have seemed as though I was stuck in the situation, which I definitely was, but after a while I knew inside that it was wrong.

Another confession I had to make was that I had voluntarily involved myself in extramarital affairs. I thought that being "the other woman" was normal because of what I'd experienced with my cousin James. My mind was set to believe that my goal in life was to please men when their wives didn't. Yes, it was an after effect of the sexual abuse, but it was something that I had to admit I had actively done, and I had to seek God for forgiveness, as well as healing. As long as I continued to make excuses for my behavior, healing could never take place. As I confronted this issue, I found comfort in I John 1:9 (KJV), *"If we confess our sins, He is faithful and just to forgive us our sins, and to cleanse us from all unrighteousness."* I understood that the preposition "if" indicated that there was a condition attached to my healing. I had to do my part before God could do His. I had to confess and no longer justify my wrong.

FORGIVENESS

I often think of forgiveness as a cure for a terminal illness. It's also a key that can unlock the door to our blessings. While forgiving is liberating, it's one of the hardest things for many of us to do.

Many think that forgiving someone means that you're telling the person that what was done to hurt you is being excused. For me, forgiving was hard because I didn't feel that my abusers deserved to be forgiven. I actually wanted God to show me grace and mercy, but I wanted Him to punish them severely. I had to apply Matthew 6:14 and 15 to my situation. I eventually understood that forgiveness is important to God, so much so that He said He would not forgive us if we refused to forgive others. Once I applied prayer and the Word of God to my situation, God taught me to see my abusers through His eyes. Once I started to view them as sons and daughters of God, I was able to forgive them and move on. Regardless of how angry I was or how hurt I had been, one thing didn't change: they were God's children, and He loved them, too.

The energy I'd exhausted reliving the pain, holding grudges, hating my abusers was shortening my life and hindering my ministry. I had to trust God to deal with my abusers in His way, and however that transpired did not need to be my concern. I had to focus on the cross and know that Jesus died so that I could be healed, and so that my abusers could be healed, also. You see, as I sought healing, I began to understand that my abusers needed healing just like I did. When individuals act out abusive behaviors, they are usually exhibiting symptoms of mental or emotional disturbances. As I mentioned, Jesus came to heal all kinds of sicknesses. Therefore, as I received the healing I desired, I began to pray that the abusers would also be healed. Once I stopped being the victim and began to be the victor, the process of forgiving empowered me to receive my healing and believe that God would also heal my abusers.

SEEK THE HELP YOU NEED

After years of trying to get through some of the emotional problems on my own, eventually I realized that I needed some professional help. While some may not need to seek professional counseling to help them get over their abuse, my case was different. While considering the kind of help you need, seek God first. My favorite scripture comes from Proverbs 3:5, 6 (KJV): ***"Trust in the Lord with all thine heart; and lean not unto thine own understanding. In all*** *thy ways acknowledge Him, and He shall direct thy paths."* While I respected the opinion of my friends, I also sought God about how to obtain my healing, and He led me to seek Christian counseling and therapy. When God tells you which route you should take, don't hesitate—move forward. Don't be discouraged by people who do not understand how you can be anointed to do God's work, but still need therapy. You must understand that your anointing is not what needs therapy—your emotions are. The same way you have a full physical every year to take care of your physical body, sometimes you need similar help to care for your mental health, as well.

DON'T GIVE UP

Therapy was very difficult for me. There were times when I didn't think I would make it, but I made a decision to stick with the treatment. This was only after the realization, however, that this was a part of God's plan for me. All that I'd been through was not just about me or for me. Eventually I learned that I had gone through these events in my life because of the many women depending on me. Though I contemplated quitting, the Holy Spirit was my best cheerleader. After one of my many decisions to discontinue therapy, I had a dream in which God showed me many houses that had no curtains in their windows. As I drove by these houses, I saw women sitting, looking hopelessly out of the windows. I could hear them saying, "Why did she give up? Now we'll never make it." When I awoke, I changed my mind and decided not to give up. I began to study Philippians 1:6 (KJV), *"Being confident of this very thing, that He which hath begun a good work in you will perform it until the day of Jesus Christ."* God had started something in me that was definitely unfinished. I understood that the process of my healing was only the beginning, and I knew that if I could just survive this part, my future would be brighter than my past and present. If you decide to attend counseling or therapy, don't give up! Someone's life could be depending on your testimony of survival.

I must be honest and tell you that undoing the damage of abuse is a long, sometimes painful process. You must be willing to patiently walk through it. Don't be fooled, as others have, into thinking that your life should be left "as is." Do not be willing to forfeit your joy. Don't make the decision to never trust or love again, just so that you can forget the pain. I believe that John 10:10 sums it up best when Jesus says, ***"...I am come that they might have life, and that they might have it more abundantly."***

Understand that it's God's desire to see us whole, prospering according to His Word. It's not God's intention for us to live in fear and distress, lacking trust and missing out on what He's promised us. Your destiny is just around the corner, beyond your healing. God knows everything about your life and what He has planned for you. Stop thinking that you are a living mistake—you're not—***you are meant to be!***

TIPS FOR PARENTS

While many therapists and psychiatrists have studied the various warning signs of sexual abuse, I would like to share some of the signs I exhibited in hopes that you will know what to look for if you are concerned that your child may be experiencing sexual abuse. In truth, many of "clinical" tell-tale warning signs were present in my case, but no one took notice.

Additionally, many parents make the mistake of misunderstanding the profile of someone who is likely to take advantage of a child sexually. They think that all pedophiles have prior criminal histories, that they abuse drugs or alcohol, or that they have been labeled a misfits by society. While some pedophiles do fall into this category, a high percentage of them are successful business people, clergy, and "outstanding citizens." Many pedophiles have direct, regular contact with the child, they've studied the child, and they have built a strong sense of trust with the child.

Anxiety

Parents should take notice if their child expresses a sudden discomfort or anxiety when a certain individual comes around. If the child has been comfortable around the individual previously and suddenly there is a concern, parents should thoroughly investigate the child's discomfort. If sexual abuse is found, parents should take the necessary action: they should contact the proper authorities to investigate. Parents should never cause the child to feel that the abuse is his or her fault. Although this is a very sensitive situation, parents should remain calm at all times and ensure security of the child who's been abused.

Bed-wetting

Some studies have shown that childhood bed-wetting can result from a child's weak bladder, nervousness, or heavy sleeping. Because I didn't fall under any of these categories, I was simply labeled as being too lazy to get out of bed at night to use the bathroom. I was a bed-wetter for an extensive period of time. Because I was so preoccupied with the abuse I was experiencing, very often I would be unable to sleep. Once I was able to finally fall asleep, my body would relax to the extent that I didn't wake up when my bladder was full. This went on until the time I entered high school at age fourteen.

Bullying/Anger/Violent Behavior

When a child feels out-of-control, betrayed, rejected, and scared, he or she may act out violently. This was one of my most prevalent signs. As a result of being sexually abused, I often became very angry. Because my abusers were aggressive and manipulative, I felt helpless in dealing with them. Therefore, I began to take out my aggression on others. I knew I was not strong enough to fight my attackers, so I took my anger out on my peers by bullying them. Not only was I a bully as a child, but as I became older I would also become very violent if I felt that one of my peers was trying to control or manipulate me. Over the years I've had to prayerfully train myself to choose my battles so that I could avoid returning to this type of behavior.

Flashbacks/Nightmares

I can't begin to count the number of times I sat in church, having flashbacks of being raped, or trying to sleep while being tormented by nightmares. Normally, when I experienced these flashbacks and nightmares they vividly brought back the pain that I'd initially felt. When I began the healing process, I found that the only solutions to this were praying and reading scriptures concerning peace to cover my mind.

Guilt and Shame

These are tools that the enemy frequently uses to defeat the children of God. Whenever a child is being abused, he or she experiences a sense of guilt because the child feels responsible for attracting the abuser's behavior. Additionally, to alleviate the guilt the abuser feels, he will place the blame on the child to make the child feel like a bad individual. The shame comes when the child is introduced to the body in a sick and unnatural manner. A child should be taught about their body parts properly, not during acts of sexual perversion. I battled with this guilt and shame until I was forty years old. No matter how other people saw me, inside I still felt horribly responsible for my abuse. It was not until I saw myself through the eyes of God that my mentality changed.

Insecurity

How can a child feel secure when someone who is called to protect them becomes his or her abuser? When a child loses trust in an adult, especially due to abuse, the child becomes insecure. Children believe that parents and other adults are there to nurture, protect, love, and guide them. When an adult steps out of this role and into the role of an abuser, it causes the child to become confused. In addition, children become insecure because they feel violated and they don't know how to voice what they feel. In such cases, the child begins to look for validation from anyone who will give them the attention that he or she needs. If not addressed during childhood, the child will become an adult who to repeatedly seeks companionship from people who have the same abusive characteristics.

Promiscuity

If the abuse continues unnoticed, the child may become promiscuous. Once a child has been exposed to sexual feelings that he or she is too young to understand, the child may begin to desire sexual gratification. This is because the craving for sex has been awakened too soon. Parents may notice that their child has begun dancing provocatively or wearing revealing clothing. The child may even become flirtatious with others, regardless of the person's age or gender. The sensual way the child walks, sits, talks, or even the way he or she stands may all be signs pointing to promiscuity.

Isolation

If the abuser is aggressive and physically abusive, the child may withdraw. Normally sexual abuse gives birth to shame, which results in self-imposed isolation. Many children who are victims of incest often experience this primarily because they're embarrassed to be around the abuser, particularly if it is someone in their immediate family. The child is often sworn to secrecy by the abuser—sometimes even threatened—to prevent from other family members from learning about the abuse.

These are just a few warning signs for parents to beware of. If you suspect sexual abuse, or if your child is experiencing any of the signs mentioned above, talk with your child to determine whether there's a problem. Your child's actions may be signs of sexual or some other type of abuse—either way, investigation is necessary. Seek help from the proper authorities and some form of counseling may be needed. Explore all information pertaining to your child's experience and needs.

I have shared my testimony in this book to prevent some young woman from having to live the nightmare that I lived. Although it was very painful, God has allowed me to walk through the process of healing, during which He turned my messes into a miracle and produced a powerful ministry. I pray for every woman who has been abused, and who has found it hard to move on. Know that healing is yours—God meant for you to be whole, healthy, and joyous! For you *are not a mistake, you ARE meant to be!*

What Others Are Saying About Evangelist Hines

"Evangelist Hines is a woman whose heart—in good and bad times—has been for God and His people. She is a true friend, sister, aunt, and a great mother. Over the years that I've known her, she has proven time and time again to be full of integrity. She is a wonderful teacher, preacher, and evangelist. In the most unselfish way, she has opened herself to inspection, as she testifies about the most personal pains, betrayals, and trials that she has endured over the course of her life. We are all blessed and our lives more enriched because of our encounter with this woman of God!"

Lynn Burrow, Author and Teacher
Christian Women for Jesus Ministries, Inc.

"From transparency to transformation! Evangelist Hines shares her testimony in exchange for her freedom. As the Bible declares in Revelation 12:11, *'And they overcame him by the blood of the Lamb, and by the word of their testimony; and they loved not their lives unto the death.'* The testimony in this book will transition you from bondage, shame, and embarrassment and will position you for freedom."

Dr. Angela Corprew-Boyd, Author and Teacher
Women Empowered in the Millennium Inc.

CPSIA information can be obtained
at www.ICGtesting.com
Printed in the USA
LVHW091937130221
679256LV00041B/370